PAUL GREEN

PAUL GREEN

North Carolina Writers on
the Legacy of the State's
Most Celebrated Playwright

EDITED BY

GEORGANN EUBANKS AND

MARGARET D. BAUER

— BLAIR —

*The mission of Blair/Carolina Wren Press is to seek out, nurture,
and promote literary work by new and underrepresented writers.*

We gratefully acknowledge the ongoing support of general operations by the
Durham Arts Council's United Arts Fund and the North Carolina Arts Council.

Library of Congress Control Number: 2024935952

To Laurence Avery,
enduring scholar and keeper of Paul Green's legacy

CONTENTS

Foreword

This collection of essays examines the life and selected works of North Carolina's most distinguished playwright of the twentieth century, Paul Eliot Green (1894–1981). The essays, commissioned by the Paul Green Foundation, come from an award-winning array of contemporary North Carolina writers who have been involved in the theater and literature communities in the state in various ways—as actors, directors, playwrights, poets, novelists, teachers, and social justice advocates. While by no means biographically comprehensive of Green's life, the essayists' frank reflections on Green's work and relationships are meant to launch new conversations about a man who was seen as progressive, even radical, in his time.

Paul Green is still remembered for his ardent advocacy for human rights, racial equity, prison reform, and ending the death penalty. He lived in an era, however, when such terms were not the popular currency of the day, particularly in the American South. His personal story—the molding of his character, his moral compass, his creative gifts, and his passion for justice—follows closely alongside the emergent struggle for dignity and equity for African Americans, Native Americans, and other people of color in the twentieth century. Green's plays were the lanterns he held up to shine light on these issues. But Green, a white man of privilege, steeped in the Jim Crow South, could not fully understand the inherited trauma, disenfranchisement, and brutality directed toward persons of color in his era. Such an awareness is still being unpacked individually and collectively by southerners with African, Indigenous, European, and other backgrounds.

Monographs, critical essays, and biographies have been written about Green and his work, though his artistic prominence as an American playwright has dimmed in recent decades. This book offers a contemporary reckoning with Green's portrayal of taboo topics that were meant primarily to challenge white theatergoers of his time. These essays ask hard questions in a present-day context about Green's relevance. It is the hope of the Paul Green Foundation that North Carolina readers of all ages who may know very little of Green's body of work or his activism will learn more about this unusual playwright. Our fundamental goal is to stimulate fresh discussions of Paul Green's legacy by examining the forces in the playwright's life and in society that shaped his writing and his progressive stance (for the time in which he lived) on human rights.

Green spent his eighty-seven years bearing witness to the habits and beliefs of rural folk in his native Harnett County, an agricultural county on the fall line between the piedmont and the coastal plain of North Carolina. From childhood forward, Green memorized the scenes, stories, and language of his neighbors. Green's people were cotton and tobacco farmers—sharecroppers and tenants, Black, white, and Native American—all driven by the seasonal rituals of groundbreaking, planting, cropping, and going to market. His neighbors and family were socially divided by the legacy of the Civil War and earlier by the genocide committed against the Indigenous peoples of the region. His mettle, like that of his neighbors, was forged in a hardscrabble landscape and climate that was, by turns, beloved and fraught.

With his mother's encouragement, Green developed a lifelong appetite for classical literature. He could quote the Bible on most any subject, though he eschewed formal religious practices. He began writing poems as a schoolboy and was tapped to serve as the teacher and principal of a grade school even before entering college. He also saved the funds he needed for college by playing semiprofessional baseball. (He was an ambidextrous pitcher.)

Ultimately, Green would ply his considerable intellectual gifts mainly in service to the stage—writing plays, screenplays, and the unique genre he invented, the symphonic drama. Because playwriting depends more heavily on dialogue than any other literary form, Green's ear became his greatest strength. He would hone this gift at the University of North Carolina at Chapel Hill (UNC) under his mentor, Professor Frederick Koch, the founder of the Carolina Playmakers theater group, which was committed to staging student plays about common folk. Koch encouraged Green to "write what you know."

Green had come to the university in 1916 bearing dark memories of the abuse and violence of his kinsmen toward their African American neighbors. He'd also witnessed the marginalization of the Coharie and Lumbee Indians in his section of the state, the latter being the largest Native American tribe east of the Mississippi. Schools in several counties around Green were segregated into three groups—white, Black, and Indian. Later in life he would protest the system in which Harnett County's Native American students had to travel seventy miles round trip to another county for high school classes. These aspects of life in eastern North Carolina made a lasting impression on him.

Unlike his younger classmate and fellow Carolina Playmaker, the vagabond novelist Thomas Wolfe, who famously declared that a writer could never go home again, Green kept to his roots. (Green was a pallbearer at Wolfe's funeral.) In his artistic output, Green never left behind what he learned as a young man about the human condition. Though his work eventually took him around the world, Harnett County was his home and his heart.

Green's first trip abroad came in 1918 as an enlisted soldier during World War I. Inspired by President Woodrow Wilson's claim that the United States was pursuing "the war to end all wars," he voluntarily interrupted his undergraduate studies to serve. After a year of basic training with the 105th Engineers, Green saw heavy combat in the trenches of Belgium and France. He did not expect to survive. A body of poems came out of his military experience, as did a lifetime of haunting nightmares.

Green returned to the university in the fall of 1919, now older than most of his classmates but determined to master the skills of playwriting and the discipline of philosophy. One of his earliest plays, *White Dresses*, was to be produced on campus at UNC but was cancelled by administrators because it addressed the topic of sexual relations between whites and people of color.

Green graduated in 1921 and began graduate school in philosophy at Carolina. He married fellow playwright Elizabeth Lay in 1922. The couple then moved to Ithaca, New York, for Paul to complete a second year of graduate study at Cornell University. Green returned to teach philosophy at UNC in the fall of 1923, while continuing to write for the stage. It would be only four years before he was awarded the Pulitzer Prize for Drama for his Broadway play *In Abraham's Bosom*. Though he took various leaves over the years to write and mount productions of his many plays and film scripts, Green remained on the faculty at UNC until his retirement in 1944.

To tell the story of Paul Green the writer is to locate him at the center of a blossoming and generous statewide literary community in North Carolina. His steady vision was catalytic. He reveled in the kinship of his fellow North Carolina writers and cheered their productivity. First as a member of the philosophy department and then as a professor of dramatic arts at UNC, Green would also correspond, collaborate, and visit with many other literary colleagues. Green was a friend to Sherwood Anderson, Erskine Caldwell, William Faulkner, Robert Frost, DuBose Heyward, Langston Hughes, Randall Jarrell, James Weldon Johnson, Romulus Linney, Clifford Odets, Maxwell Perkins, Carl Sandburg, and Thornton Wilder, among many others.

As this twentieth-century literary roll call suggests, female and Black writers were fewer and often marginalized in his era, but Green welcomed their company. Beyond encouraging scores of student writers at the University of North Carolina, he became a kind of literary magnet, coaching aspiring and accomplished writers who came to the Chapel Hill campus to work with him, notably Betty Smith (author of *A Tree Grows in Brooklyn*), the folklorist and novelist Zora Neale Hurston (who was the first African American to integrate Green's writing group on campus), the Mexican novelist and playwright Josefina Niggli, and the Mississippi-born novelist Richard Wright, who asked Green to collaborate with him on the Broadway adaptation of Wright's novel, *Native Son*.

Green's story also extends to Broadway, beginning during the Harlem Renaissance. His early determination to write serious parts for Black actors was groundbreaking for nearly exclusively white audiences and therefore challenging for many theaters to support. Nevertheless, Green's play *In Abraham's Bosom* gave voice to the troubles and aspirations of a Black man in 1927. As the son of a formerly enslaved woman and a white plantation owner, protagonist Abraham McCranie tried and failed to create a successful school for Black children in the rural South. Green's theme of intimate, cross-racial relationships and their consequences would continue through his most serious work, including his next Broadway play, *The House of Connelly*, which he began writing in 1926. The play was first published and produced in 1931.

Later, with the Depression in full swing, Green wrote and published two novels that were considered for screenplay adaptation in Hollywood. Green sold the film rights to *The Laughing Pioneer* (1932) and argued that the mysterious Greta Garbo would be the perfect actress for the lead. His second novel, *This Body the Earth* (1935), bears witness to the lives of white sharecroppers vying with formerly enslaved families struggling to survive after Reconstruction. Though neither novel was adapted for the screen, Green's writing skills turned out to be in high demand in Hollywood, beginning in 1932.

With a growing family to support and the promise of lucrative contracts, Green took a leave from UNC (from 1931 to 1938) and worked off and on in California writing scripts for popular movies starring such actors as Bette Davis, Janet Gaynor, Errol Flynn, Fred MacMurray, and Will Rogers, among others. He was employed by Fox, Warner Brothers, and M.G.M., but ultimately his disillusionment with the medium of popular film and its craven business ethos brought him back to North Carolina.

According to Green's daughter Janet, the short story writer Katherine Anne Porter once said of Green in Hollywood, "The honest, tender and gifted soul stood out like a stalk of good sugar cane in a thicket of poison ivy" (qtd. in Warren n.p.). The two films for which he is best known were stories of rural farming families: *Cabin in the Cotton* and *State Fair*. The latter received an Oscar nomination for Best Picture in 1933.

It was during his Hollywood years that Green first took a firm stand against the death penalty in North Carolina, albeit from a distance, writing to various political correspondents and opinion leaders about capital cases in the state and the highly publicized incident involving the "Scottsboro Boys" in Alabama. It was during this period as well that he hosted the poet Langston Hughes on the UNC campus, to the dismay of many in the Chapel Hill community. He also called out university leaders for not allowing African American day laborers access to books in the university library that they were building. In 1936, Green's new, one-act play, *Hymn to the Rising Sun,* produced by New York's City Repertory Theatre, illustrated the tragic practice of prisoner abuse in chain gangs, another blight on society that Green would work to abolish.

Throughout the 1930s, Green was racing back and forth across the country as his third major play, *Johnny Johnson,* which the producers initially promoted as a comic antiwar musical, was in development by the Group Theatre in New York, the same company that had first staged *The House of Connelly* on Broadway in 1931. It was the first time the playwright collaborated with an internationally recognized composer, German-born Kurt Weill, who had created the music for *The Threepenny Opera,* written by playwright Bertolt Brecht and produced for the German stage in 1928. The character Johnny Johnson drew heavily on the horrors Green experienced as a soldier in the Great War, and the play is considered by many to be Green's most durable work.

During Green's childhood, music had been ever present in the Green household. His mother sang and taught her son to play the organ. He also taught himself as a youth to play the violin. The power of folk music to raise the emotional stakes in a scene had already been deployed in several of Green's earlier plays, and the experience of crafting *Johnny Johnson* with Kurt Weill played an inspirational role in his next project: a commission to write a commemorative drama about North Carolina's "Lost Colony" to be presented on the shores of the Outer Banks.

Green intuitively understood the importance of place in the shaping of community identity and loyalty, which was the genius behind the new theatrical genre he conceived in 1936. He had immersed himself in the pageantry of opera and attended European folk plays during his Guggenheim Fellowships in Germany and England in 1928 and 1929. These experiences also contributed to his first outdoor symphonic drama, *The Lost Colony.* In 1937, a month after its July 4 premiere, President Franklin Roosevelt and First Lady Eleanor Roosevelt attended a performance at Fort Raleigh on Roanoke Island, to great national fanfare. To this day, amateur and professional actors come together annually to stage performances throughout the summer at the site of the 1587 English settlement south of Jamestown, Virginia. Here the first English child born in what is now North Carolina mysteriously disappeared along with her mother and a group of settlers and their Indigenous neighbors. Green recognized immediately that the power of his play would be amplified by its presentation on the same shifting sands where his characters — Native American and English — first met and struggled together to survive.

The Lost Colony marked another turn in Green's work. In the years that followed and up until his death, he would be in demand across the country, visiting communities that wanted to transform their local history into musical theater. Green's grand theatrical form generally demanded an outdoor setting, dazzling dances and chorale pieces, elaborate costumes and lighting, and scores of actors and singers.

In the 1940s, Green gave up his faculty position at UNC and was able to travel more freely across the country to examine potential outdoor drama sites. He hiked in the woods of Ohio and Kentucky, in the lowland scrub of Georgia and Louisiana, in rocky Texas canyons, on the historic site of Williamsburg, Virginia, alongside Rock Creek in Washington, D.C., and in the Florida heat of St. Augustine. He would walk off the footprint for amphitheaters to be constructed in advance of each play's premiere. In the end Green wrote seventeen historical plays that were performed seasonally across the country for various runs. He also coached a cadre of younger playwrights who adopted his recipe for the genre of symphonic outdoor drama and made it their own. According to Paul Green scholar Laurence G. Avery, there were between thirty-five and fifty historical plays — Green's and others' — running in any given summer in the United States toward the beginning of the twenty-first century, attracting tourism dollars and boosting local economies.

In spite of his many artistic projects, Green worked assiduously during the latter half of his life to gather support for prisoners facing the death penalty. He denounced the segregation of schools and colleges, the grim threat of nuclear proliferation, the scourge of poverty, and the horrible losses in the Vietnam War.

He also became a nationally recognized champion of the arts. He was active in several national arts organizations and conferences. With his mentee, the novelist John Ehle, he helped to launch the North Carolina School of the Arts (a state-funded multidisciplinary conservatory for high school and college talent). Green was a founder of the North Carolina Symphony, the first state-funded orchestra in the nation. As a member of the U.S. National Commission for UNESCO (United Nations Educational, Scientific and Cultural Organization) from 1950 to 1952, Green and his daughter Betsy traveled to Paris for UNESCO's Sixth General Conference.

In 1963, during the early heat of the civil rights movement, Green took up screenwriting once more, without credit, to work on the film adaptation of the bestselling *Black Like Me*, a searing memoir by white journalist John Howard Griffin, who chemically changed his skin color and traveled across the segregated South posing as a Black man. At the same time Green was invited to take a post as a visiting professor in UNC's relatively new Department of Radio, TV, and Motion Pictures, the first of its kind in the nation. This appointment put Green in a high-profile position to protest on behalf of UNC System President William Friday. Green condemned the controversial "Speaker Ban," a ruling by the North Carolina legislature that prohibited Communists from speaking to any assembly on the university campus. Green remained an outspoken defender of freedom of speech, civil rights, and other humanitarian causes until his death in 1981.

In addition to his literary works, Green—ever the documentarian of everyday folk—left behind an enormous collection of diaries, reminiscences, letters, opinion pieces, essays, and a hefty, two-volume encyclopedia of folk sayings collected over his lifetime on pocket-sized cards.

Green pulled few punches in his personal papers and let loose in his letters when necessary to make his point with the powerful. His attitudes toward war and discrimination, toward the plight of prisoners and the poor came from the stories and scenes he remembered from his lived experience and then revisited over and over in his fertile mind. Understanding Green's frustrations and the satisfactions that came with his writing projects may prove to be of continuing value to aspiring writers in North Carolina, particularly those interested in creating characters for the stage that further validate and extend the profile of an increasingly diverse American society. As long as we understand the theater to be a place where we hold up a mirror to our culture—its foibles and affirmations—we continue the work to which Paul Green aspired.

PAUL GREEN

Bearing Witness

The Harnett County of Paul Green's Childhood

Paul Green and my maternal grandparents were from the same generation, growing up on rural farms in eastern North Carolina in the early 1900s. Though sixty miles apart, they would have shared sunrise and set, hot humid summers, a wealth of pecan trees, and wide cotton and tobacco fields stretching out before them. They knew the same railroad line and river basin, the Cape Fear, that ran through their landscape. They also shared an area rife with racial prejudice and tensions.

But Paul Green differed from my grandparents and so many others growing up in this part of the world at that time. He not only absorbed stories and details of local lives and racial discrimination, but went on to re-create them in his writings, bringing a deep level of awareness to the surface. He had a keen sense of social justice and of right and wrong. The many vivid scenes he put forward in his work stand as proof of a region steeped in racial hatred and hypocrisy. The frightening truths he witnessed as a child were further complicated by the confusing actions of the adults around him. How could a caring relative also be someone capable of committing racial violence or denouncing another human's worth?

Many of Green's images pull me right back to my own childhood in southeastern North Carolina. I was interested in knowing all I could about my maternal grandmother's childhood. I spent a lot of time with her, and she seemed to enjoy telling stories and painting a detailed portrait: dirt yards swept clean; a hole in the corner of the room of the house so the floor could be washed out; well water and boiling washpots; hog killings and the many steps that went into frying a chicken, from wringing the neck to bleeding, scalding, plucking, cutting, and frying. My grandmother said

that the business of preparing the chicken was why she never felt like eating it. She told how it was so exciting when Santa Claus left an orange and
some pecans in her sock or shoebox at Christmas and how the houses were
built up off the ground so there was cool dark space below.

Both of my parents talked about playing under the house as children,
especially in the summer when it was hot. They remembered building "frog
houses," something my grandmother had also recalled. The method was a
simple one. You covered your foot with a mound of dirt and packed and
patted it down solid. Then, with the greatest care and ease, you slipped your
foot out to leave a little cave. My sister and I would do this on summer trips
to the beach, only to return later to find little things left in there—a shell
or a coin—while our parents described the frog who had hopped by to visit.
I have tried periodically over the years to look up any mention or origin of
these dirt "frog houses" but with no success. None of my friends had grown
up building them—had ever even heard of them—but then, the familiar
image appeared when I read Paul Green's first essay in the collection *Home
to My Valley* called "Rassie and the Barlow Knife":

> I was out in front of my father's house playing in the flat and sand-
> clogged water ditch. I was small enough to be wearing some sort of a
> dress then but big enough already to be about my own business which
> was the making of a frog house. This dirt house was made by burrow-
> ing one bare foot in the sand and piling the damp dirt carefully patted
> and packed over and around and then at the proper time gently pulling
> the foot out and leaving a snug little cave for any homeseeking frog. (3)

This innocent image of childhood opened a door for me, not only into
Green's heartbreaking memories of his playmate, but also into the atmosphere of my grandmother's world in the early 1900s.

Green's essay goes on to describe meeting Rassie McLeod, the Black son
of a tenant farmer, who became his inseparable friend until Rassie died at
age ten of typhoid fever. Rassie and Paul built frog houses together. Rassie
taught Paul how to pop his finger joints, drive imaginary horses, make
a beanshooter out of a dogwood branch, and how to spit tobacco juice
between his front teeth. Clearly this early friendship and the grief Green

Paul Green's childhood home still stands in Harnett County, North Carolina. Photo by Donna Campbell, courtesy of the photographer.

experienced when Rassie lost his life shaped the author's view of the world and the contradictory actions of the grown-ups in his world.

The doctor in Green's story who was tending to the sick family blames the poor conditions of Rassie's family on Paul Green's father, the same man who had laughed and thought it was fine for young Paul to spend the night at his friend's sharecropper shack. Paul's older half sister had already been going to nurse the family in their sickness. She even washes Rassie's naked body in death and asks Paul for his nightshirt for Rassie to be buried in—and yet, we have already heard her racist judgments and utterances about Rassie's kin prior to this event. Paul's father builds the coffin, the sister fixes the cloth within, and Paul and his father dig the grave.

Paul asks, "Ain't you going to say something over him, Papa?" Green goes on to tell of his father's reaction: "My father hesitated a moment, pulled off his hat, and then murmured out a few words in the thickening gloom. . . . But he said nothing about Rassie's being in Heaven, for like a great many folks in North Carolina at that time he was still a bit uncertain as to whether Negroes really had full-fledged souls and would be allowed in Heaven" (15).

Unlike his father, Green believes that Rassie *is* in Heaven, and he plants a stick for a grave marker. He comes back the next day to carve the words: *Rassie—he sleeps here.* The knife he used to make the letters had belonged to Rassie, who asked as he lay dying that it be given to Paul. For Green, the object remained symbolic of the friendship, and probably a vestige of the messages he was receiving from the world around him. We learn that when Paul returns years later, the grave has been plowed under. No sign was left of the monument to his friend.

Green often delivers such information as cold, hard fact that though we might crave more judgment, none is required. The juxtaposition of these observations—what was right and what was wrong, what his father does and does not do—is clear. I came away from Green's stories feeling that they were *more* powerful without the writer's summations and judgments. Green puts his readers in the position of witness. We are left to our own realizations and conclusions. We have seen and heard what so many have chosen *not* to see or acknowledge in those times and in our own.

———————

Many of my grandmother's stories centered on the milestones recorded at the front of her Bible—the births and the deaths within her family. She told how her father had died young; in fact, when I looked it up, I realized he died around the same time that Rassie did. Her identical twin died in 1899, when they were only two, which would have been right after the Wilmington, North Carolina, massacre—a violent murderous attack on the Black community by white supremacists—and a time of brewing racial violence in Robeson County, as well. Did she know this? I wonder. Surely her parents would have.

She had another sister who "perished" at age eleven when she stopped eating. That was the whole story my grandmother told, leaving us to wonder what medical condition might have been responsible. Instead, the focus of my grandmother's story was how her mother went and sat by her sister's grave every day, crying and grieving, until one day a big storm blew up. She said that the thunder boomed, and lightning struck right near her feet. She ran home, terrified, saying that God had spoken to her. God had told her to go home and tend to the living.

I have visited those three family graves, each marked in a tiny plot of land, long sold away, out in the country surrounded by someone else's farmland. Still, unlike Rassie McLeod's grave, their places have been honored and not plowed under.

"My mother was a clown," my grandmother often said, "always cutting up and acting like a child herself." This preface usually led to how my grandmother did much of the work around the house and was more of a mother to her younger sister than their own mother was. She explained that when she was a young girl, there was a man who helped on several of the local farms and that all the children loved him, including her mother, who thought he was very funny. She said that people called him "Nigger Bill." She whispered the name, even though she had always told us never to use that word and that it was not a nice thing to say. Generally, she used the word *Negro*, sometimes *colored*, but when she told that story, she used the name he had been called. What made her mother laugh so much, my grandmother said, was when Bill explained how most people liked to sleep with their heads out and their feet covered but that he liked to have his head covered and his feet out.

My grandmother laughed and said, "Everybody loved him." In the same breath she said, "and it was awful what happened." When pressed, she told me that Bill was murdered and left out in the field behind a potato hill. I asked who murdered him, and she said no one knew, that it was so sad. Like so many of her stories, that one ended abruptly and was assigned to the unknown.

That is the only murder that my grandmother ever told me about—and perhaps it's the only one that directly touched her life in that rural place. Still, the cruel and evil history we now know would suggest that a story like my grandmother's would have been only one of an overwhelming number of violent acts of hatred committed against people of color. She had other stories of people she might call a ne'er-do-well—drunkard, lazy, thief—and whenever I asked what happened to them, she often replied, "I don't know, but I bet he went to Texas." I suspect some did, but I also would suspect that just as many lingered on with no consequences for their actions in daylight or under the cloak of night.

Green presents and studies the lack of action or consequence in the lives of adults witnessing cruel injustices in many of his memories. In an interview with James R. Spence, Green tells of a relative who stops his work in the field to throw a water dipper to the ground and "stamp it into shapelessness" (qtd. in Spence 17). Just before, Rassie's father had used the dipper to get a drink. The relative proclaimed that no white person could drink after a Black tenant farmer. Green goes on to suggest that the man was "no doubt satisfied in one way with himself, but being a human being, a spiritual being, I'm sure there was some spiritual discomfort even so" (qtd. in Spence 17). I think Green was more generous in imagining his relative's inner life than contemporary readers would have been. His writings carry a strand of optimistic hope that men would recognize their wrongs, but there are other incidents that don't leave much room for hope.

In "Excursion," another sketch in the collection *Home to My Valley*, Green describes an incident he witnessed at a train depot in Angier, North Carolina. A train had stopped at the station, and one of the cars was filled with Black students. Their well-dressed teacher stepped down onto the platform to ask when the train would reach Durham. From Green's point of view, all that was clear in that moment was the anger of the white engineer who told the man that it was none of his business. When the teacher politely said that he didn't mean any harm, the anger heightened, and the engineer grabbed a stick and hit the teacher in the face. Green told Rhoda Wynn during an interview, "My father had come up there and stopped and was standing there . . . and he didn't say anything. He was just staring at the Negro's bloody face. And the Negro teacher—all he said to the engineer was, 'Cap'n, you done ruin't my shirt' " (VII-55). Green said he watched the train pull away with the teacher and his students back in the "Jim Crow car," the "little children sitting straight and immobile and the schoolteacher in the front of the car with his head bowed over and his still-bloody handkerchief against his face" (VII-56).

In another tale told to oral historian Billy E. Barnes, Green remembers a boarder named Moody who lived in the Green home and disclosed to young Paul that he wouldn't be working his sawmill that day because he was going to a lynching. The language the man used to explain this was hateful and violent. When Moody got back to the Green house later that evening, he expressed his disappointment. He said he arrived at the hanging too late. All he could do was add some bullets to the dead man. It's a shocking, terrible story and no doubt stood as an example of the kind of memory that pushed Green to his life as a social activist.

I think it is important to note that Green lays out these memories in ways that might invite the reader to qualify degrees of the injustices: a water dipper ruined, hitting a man for no reason, contributing to a lynching. What is notably consistent, however, are those like Green's father who don't react and are guilty in their complacent passivity: these extreme cases are easy to recognize, but it seems clear to me that Green was also deeply haunted by the huge swath of gray occupied by those who witnessed, knew better, and did nothing. Did their lack of action mean they shared the hatred? It is hard to read these pieces and not step back with a kind of sick amazement that we still ask these same questions after witnessing contemporary incidents of racially motivated violence.

––––––––––

Green's awareness of his father's observations of such events without response paints a disturbing, complicated portrait, and one that implicates the state at large. The child, Paul, was receiving mixed messages even in his earliest years. His father allowed him to go to Rassie's house (something many white children would not have been allowed to do). At the same time, he learns from the local doctor that his father did not take care of the house Rassie lived in. When he was questioned about the conditions, Green's father spoke with a generalized stereotype to explain: "I've grown up with tenants, worked with 'em, lived with 'em and you can't change 'em," the elder Green says (*Home* 9).

In his essay about his playmate Rassie McLeod, Green remembers his eagerness to spend the night at his friend's house only to find himself feeling out of place and wanting to go back home. Both families laughed at Paul's emotional response. Green could not have articulated it at the time, but he clearly knew there were differences between the households that he did not understand.

Perhaps the inconsistency in the words and actions of the adults in Paul Green's life is a universal story. It certainly has been a struggle for me in understanding the community that raised me. There were people I was taught to admire and respect—deacons in the church, teachers, prominent upstanding citizens with the lineage to prove it—and they had been to college, they were professionals. But they told racist jokes and used the *N* word. We heard rumors of connections to the Klan. And yet they were polite to the people of color who worked for and waited on them; these individuals were *just like family*, as the saying goes, and were always included in family weddings and funerals. But my people were shocked if people of color tried to attend a particular church or class without a family-connected invitation. It is that level of hypocrisy that I think so many of us are aware of or have become aware of, and all the adages like *practice what you preach* come to mind along with excuses like *they prefer it this way*. I can't imagine any white person growing up in the South *without* some shame to bear, something said or thought or accepted. We can all plead ignorance once. And then ever after, it's a choice, a *chosen ignorance.*

So many writers have now mined the history and the facts such that it is getting harder and harder to imagine the plea of "ignorance." The work of writer Philip Gerard, historians David Cecelski and Timothy Tyson has brought much of this state's violent and racist history to the surface. Cecelski wrote a whole essay that focused on the function of the "Red Shirts" in my native county, how the Lumberton White Supremacy Club was thriving in 1900. They hosted a march with hundreds of people attending. The club provided a barbecue dinner for five hundred. Unlike members of the Klan, these citizens chose to show their faces proudly, wanting people to know who they were and what they stood for. And who were they? Cecelski begins by explaining who they were *not:*

> Rowdies and ruffians they were not. None were poor or working class. None were tradesmen, clerks, tenant farmers or farm laborers. None were women, and of course none were African American. I do not believe that any of the 21 were Croatan (Lumbee) Indian, the native people that made up 30 to 40% of Robeson County's population at that time.

Cecelski goes on to list the twenty-one members of the White Supremacy Club that he was able to identify, all prominent members of the community. One was chairman of the board of deacons of the Baptist Church; others were bankers, lawyers, and a future governor. These were the white-collar, affluent members of society, and they were sending a message to the population at large. To openly claim that they were members of the Lumberton White Supremacy Club says it all.

Did I know any of this growing up? No. Did I hear stories about it? No. Was my grandmother aware that this had happened? Her older brothers? My great-grandfather? I don't know.

The blurred lines and frightening assumptions of what makes *a good man* allow horrifying situations to go unchecked. Perhaps this, too, is a universal situation as old as Good and Evil. Certainly Gerard, Cecelski, and Tyson have done excellent work, unearthing and shining a light on the violent chapters of North Carolina's history of racism, but in his own way, of his own time, so did Paul Green, simply by staging the events on the page. He was an award-winning playwright. He understood the drama he was putting forward and knew the impact that he might have on the reader.

Green's nonfiction story of "Uncle Reuben and the Ku Klux Klan" is violent and disturbing, but it ends so neatly, just a few beats short of "happily ever after." And yet, it was the one in *Home to My Valley* that I could not stop thinking about. It was the narrative I found just as disturbing as the one about Moody, the man hungry to attend a lynching—and then even more disturbing. Moody was firmly voicing his hatred, but the circumstances for Uncle Reuben were not so easily recognized and defined.

The essay begins with young Paul noticing scars on the arms of Reuben Bailey, a Black man working in the fields. Reuben says to him, "You notice things, don't you?" (*Home* 61), and then Reuben decides that Paul is old enough to hear his story, a story that no one—not even Paul's father—would talk about. Reuben explains that once he had his freedom, the Ku Klux Klan came after him. They came to his door, and Reuben told them, "I'll kill the first man that breaks down my door" (62). But they didn't listen, they came in, and Reuben took an axe and killed the first man in. But in the process, Reuben got shot by another intruder who then stood over him and shot him several times. When Paul asked if he knew who shot him, Reuben answered yes but said he would not tell.

It's a rich, dramatic moment. Reuben decides Paul is old enough to
hear the truth and reveals his honest anger and willingness to kill in self-
defense. He knows who tried to kill him but refuses to say. Then we meet
Uncle Heck, a man Paul professes to love, a dandy of a man "all dressed
out in his white linen suit and Panama hat and swinging his gold-headed
cane" (64). Uncle Heck was the postmaster in Wilmington. The reader's
suspicion about Heck, who enters the scene at just the right moment, raises
the tension as does the dialogue that follows. Heck says to Reuben, "You
old black scoundrel, you ain't aged a day since last year," and Reuben replies
with "And you . . . look like sump'n stepped out of the bandbox of heaven,
always a spick and span gentleman" (65).

Of course, the scene goes where we are thinking it will. Reuben main-
tains his commitment not to reveal the name of who shot him, even as
Heck pushes, asking, did he tell you who shot him? Reuben interrupts
to say, "Now Mr. Heck, you know I know better'n that" (66). Heck eventually laughs and reveals himself to be the shooter. Though it comes as
no real surprise. What is a surprise is the way Reuben—the angry and
energetic Reuben who was willing to kill in self-defense and wanted Paul
to hear his story—becomes entirely submissive to Uncle Heck. Heck tells
Reuben it is the anniversary of the day he was shot, and Reuben ends up
kissing his hand and the two go off together arm in arm. Green ends the
piece with this description: "cronies, bosom buddies in these latter days.
Ah Lord!" (67).

I wasn't sure how to read that ending at first, but I choose to weigh in on
the side of irony, given what Green delivered so beautifully in the dialogue
and the strong voice of Reuben growing thinner and thinner until he was
easily manipulated into the mold of what was acceptable to Heck: the *yassir,
massah* stereotype. I would love to know what, if anything, Green might've
expressed about Heck in later years.

Green's language is often confined to the years of his own life as well as
to a white audience—making it impossible for some of his work to find
a comfortable place in today's culture—and yet, the passion he brought
to his work and the recognition of right and wrong left for the reader to

examine remains. Though the presentation might be limited—even offensive in present day—he *did* recognize injustice and went forward in his
adult life trying to shine a light on it: opposing the death penalty for the
many wrongly sentenced to death row and writing about his opposition to
it. It is easy to take a character like Heck and know where he would fit in
the write-ups about the Red Shirts. Green successfully painted the social
divisions we are still witnessing—red hats instead of red shirts and rallies
instead of barbecue dinners. His language might be outdated, and he often
keeps it all framed like a short act or a parable, but still, the truth is present.
As the writer Brian Morton explains so eloquently in an op-ed he wrote for
the *New York Times*:

> It's as if we imagine an old book to be a time machine that brings the
> writer to us. We buy a book and take it home, and the writer appears
> before us, asking to be admitted into our company. If we find that
> the writer's views are ethnocentric or sexist or racist, we reject the
> application, and we bar his or her entry into the present. . . . I think
> we'd all be better readers if we realized that it isn't the writer who's the
> time traveler. It's the reader. When we pick up an old novel, we're not
> bringing the novelist into our world and deciding whether he or she is
> enlightened enough to belong here; we're journeying into the novelist's
> world and taking a look around.

For me, having grown up so close to Harnett County, I now have a better understanding of the world of my grandmother and parents, thanks to
Green. In my own childhood, I witnessed the white flight to private schools
at the onset of integration. I can recall kids on the playground in fifth grade
saying they were for George Wallace. At the time, what did it mean beyond
the faded letters saying COLORED on a door at the movie theater? Unfortunately, so much of what Paul Green witnessed in his life continues today.
Green's work reminds us of the power of those early childhood memories,
and the images he left us with stand as proof of the many injustices that
existed then. He never forgot his boyhood friend, Rassie McLeod, and the
love that he felt at such an early age. I like to think that it was the combina-
tion of his awareness of truth and the many cruel wrongs inflicted, coupled
with his love and devotion to his young friend that paved the way for his

life as an artist and a fierce activist for social justice. Green strived to use his voice at a time when many remained passive—the inaction itself an act of submission to racism. He could have easily stayed within the limits of Harnett County, pretended that he did not see and recognize the injustices. But he did see, and he did remember, the stories and images working as portals, opening and tunneling to another time and place and sadly uncovering circumstances that still exist today. If some of the work—the language and depictions—fails to translate in our present day, it does not diminish the fact that Green's willingness to bear witness has successfully documented the time and place of his lifetime.

Education South

I t was a balmy day in spring and a funeral was going on in the Negro section of the cemetery close by the University wall. And there before the open grave amid her neighbors stood a tall middle-aged mulatto woman, mother of the dead young man to be buried. Her black cotton-gloved hands were clasped tightly down in front of her. And she gazed motionless and gaunt-eyed at the coffin resting on two chairs across from her, in which all her hopes and dreams were shut forever. No tears fell from her eyes, nor did any sound of grief or pain come through her bloodless and ash dry lips.

And the grieving song of the mourners gathered there went softly out across the spring-blossomed campus. Among the ancient leafing green trees it went and among the great gray buildings and the red brick ones and across the quiet village, gently troubling in its vibration the bees and dirtdaubers and butterflies as they sucked and played at the tender white clover in the wide commons and lawn.

The drowsy students slumped about in their chairs in the Memorial Library heard it, yawned and went on trying to concentrate on their collateral reading. And in the sleepy classrooms it was the same — if PR equals SW what is the value of V? — If economics is a science what are the categories for the filling and satisfying of human desires? — What do the Gestalt psychologists mean when they say that phenomena are more than the sum of their parts? — Wherein does the baroque differ from the classical, whether in art or literature?

And some of the stray professors and students passing along Washington Street stopped, listened a moment, and continued their easy discursive walk toward the post office. And other citizens, stopping a moment in springtime sociability over the impending bond issue for paving this same street, grew silent, took in the protruding fact of a funeral in the distance and resumed their pro and con. A Negro funeral in the cemetery there was a common thing and had been for a hundred and fifty years. And good Negro singing was common too, as well as preaching.

And down in Professor Rochambeau DeRossett's garden an old Negro plowman too stopped his mule Reuben and listened to the mighty funeral hymn of the Negroes blown along on the gentle southwest wind. He stood with grave and high-nostriled blackamoor face, his eyes thoughtful, in which little sparks of musical delight began to show. He had wanted to attend that funeral and help with the singing. He knew they'd have a good singing and good preaching at it. And besides, he had known the dead young man and his mother's high hopes for him. But 'Fessor DeRossett said be here and fix his garden, for already it was time that early sass was ready to be cut. He's been away out west on a mountain where they had a 'scope thing to look through and measure the stars, and was late in getting back to his vegetable planting. Well, anyhow, when a 'fessor said do a thing, a man better do it, for no telling when a fellow might need a friend, a good white friend in the hour of trouble, when trouble comes, as it said in the song. And nobody could be better than a 'fessor from the University. For such 'fessors, as everybody knew, were the most powerful men of all from far and roundabout.

"Giddup, giddup," the old man urged his mule Reuben, his voice softened down in respect to the grief and woe yonder in the distance. "Giddup, giddup," he said again, jerking and jiggling the line the while. And finally like breathing, Reuben leaned his ancient raw bony body, poor as quilting frames, against the collar, and the rickety Boy-Dixie plow crinkled the shallow swelling ground. Then *pyang*—and the loose-hung plowpoint struck a buried rock and broke clean off. The old plowman chet-chetted with his lips and gave out a few dad-dang-its over his usual bad luck. Still, no help for it, and he would plow no more today. A fact was a fact, and an accident was an accident. 'Fessor couldn't blame him for leaving. And tomorrow would be another day. So he turned Reuben's head into Miz DeRossett's flaming pirus–japonica hedge and hurried off in long strides toward the graveyard, his tall African kingly form moving levelly along. He began humming with his powerful bass as he went, joining tunefully in with the funeral singing. He sang his dominant, dropping down easily to low C good and strong—

> The earth in dust and ashes hid
> Before the awful sign,
> The moon ran down in purple stream
> The sun forebore to shine—
> Then grieve, grieve, grieve,
> For death's a hard trial.

He went on by the old Episcopal church, ivy-wrapped and haunted by chattering sparrows.

And inside the church young Reverend Walter Hanes, dressed in his black cassock, was intently and fervently holding his class for the Bishop who would be there tomorrow for the Sunday confirmation. Through the tall chancel windows the light fell upon his slender figure, staining it in crimson and blue and splotching along the floor and on the pupils' heads all glorified.

"How many parts are there in a sacrament?" he persuasively and sweetly inquired of the young boys and girls. And they all quoted in unison, "Two, the outward and visible sign, and the inward and spiritual grace."

"What is the outward visible sign or form in baptism?"

"Water, wherein the person is baptized, in the Name of the Father and of the Son and of the Holy Ghost."

Mr. Hanes turned and pulled a little side window quietly closed to shut out the sounds floating in from the Negro graveyard. "The distant tumult and the grieving," he said shyly. He went gently on. "What is the inward and spiritual grace, Kenan? Suppose you tell us."

And Professor Allison Haywood's little son looked thoughtfully before him and began to make answer—"A death unto sin, and a new birth unto righteousness: for being by nature born in sin, and the children of wrath, we are hereby made the children of grace." Young Mr. Hanes looked his appreciation at Kenan and for an instant glimpsed in his mind far ahead a bit of bright future for this little lad.

"I don't hear 'em singing in the graveyard now," Kenan suddenly said.

"No, we don't hear them now," said Hanes. "And you, Willene, what is required of persons to be baptized?"

And Willene Blount, daughter of Dr. Phillip Pressmore Blount, President of the University, bent her tiny head in confusion while Kenan looked protectingly and lovingly at her. Finally a mouselike running little answer of "Repentance whereby — they forsake sin — and faith so they believe — the promises of God —" came out of her lips.

Young Reverend Mr. Hanes listened pleasantly and happily as he stared out through the little window at the tender greenery of the campus, still hearing the now faint singing of the Negroes in the distance. He stood and listened, and quietly wondered. A moment he stood and listened so, then lifted the prayerbook and began reading, "Jesus came and spake unto them, saying, all power is given unto me in heaven and in earth. Go ye therefore, and make disciples —"

And out over the quiet university campus the funeral singing continued, filtering in through the doors and windows into professors' offices, the dean's sanctum, the president's office, the laboratories, and into the basements of the different buildings. And the Negro janitors stopped pushing their brooms along the halls for a while to listen. They would have been at the funeral, too, but this was a young outside fellow being buried there and they couldn't afford to use up one of their rare leave days to attend. There would be enough of their own folks dying and being buried as time passed.

And through the open windows of the classrooms where the young white men, the keepers of tomorrow and the burgeoning South, were being trained in the way they should go, the music drifted —

The bells of death ring in the night
To wake men to their doom,
Bright sparkles in the churchyard shine
To light them to their tomb —
Then grieve, grieve, grieve,
For death's a hard trial —

And the young teacher of Philosophy 16, Larry Patterson, a recent PhD from Yale, stared out over his class of some dozen young men in Logical Principles and fixed his heavy–spectacled eye upon a troubled student named Maybanks who sat blinking in the air and gulping helplessly as the words bombarded him. "I will repeat the question," said Patterson. "You may remember," he said, "at least I hope you remember, that the subject we are trying to discuss deals with what *is* versus what ought to be. Now I ask you, Mr. Maybanks, or rather do you think so—that whatever is is what ought to be; or should what *is* be improved upon?—Or in other words, is there a dichotomy—a Greek word meaning a division, a cutting, a cleavage— and again I remind you that Greek is a language all of us should give part of our time to acquaint ourselves with—yes, in other words, is there a dichotomy, a division, a separation, a difference between the actual and the moral world? Do you get the question?—Between the actually existing world that is, I say, and the one that morally ought to be?"

His big bulbous, near-sighted eye, slightly derisive, and slightly sardonic, dug deeply into the flinching soul of Mr. Maybanks who wagged his head, shuffled his big Carolina plowman's feet and in a halting voice confessed he didn't quite get the question—sir. Professor Patterson sucked in a lungful of air, slid down the window and in the quieter room now said he would repeat the question. "Pardon the interruption from the outside," he added. And Maybanks pushed his gaze out through the window and on over to the alumni building. A red-headed sapsucker was sitting on one of the chimneys, and he fastened his helpless gaze on the bird and held it there as Professor Patterson began again.

And beneath the bird in Room 203 Professor Mangum Barrett, a little spry, gray-faced man was stepping up and down in front of his Greek literature class "riding" a ministerial student by the name of Ferrell. "*Hos ephato klaion epi de stenachonto politai,*" he was intoning fiercely. And Brother Ferrell, planning to be a missionary to far away China and a master of the Septuagint some day stared at his page of Homer in grim swelling silence. "Translate, translate," Professor Barrett pleaded.

"So spake he—so spake he," stammered Ferrell, and then his words drowned in helpless silence again. Professor Barrett shook down his spotless cuffs and finger gripped them against the butt of his tobacco-stained hands, turned and with a sudden soft southern drawl went on gently and persuasively, "Go ahead, Mr. Ferrell."

"And thereunto the townspeople, the townspeople—" stammered Ferrell, and once more the faint trickle of his learning died in the sands of his vast ignorance.

Professor Barrett reached over and took the book from Ferrell's rawboned hands. Stepping back he pulled the window abstractedly but bangingly down, and leaning against the wall in the quietness began to read. "So spake he, wailing, and all of the men of the city made moan with him— *Troesin d'Hekabe hadinou exerche gooio.*" He stopped, his face easing, tasting deeply within himself the beauty of Homer and the glory and vitality of a civilization dead. "And Hekabe led in the wild lament. My child, alas my child, wherever should I live in my sore anguish now thou art perished who wast my boast both night and day in the city and a blessing to all."

And so Professor Barrett went on reading Greek and, as was his wont, took time out to berate our present civilization awhile, especially the poor deluded and misguided South, and to pay his fealty to another. He compared the foolish lament and grieving for the dead out there in the cemetery near the wall with the beautiful and mighty sorrow of the ancient Greeks.

And abruptly he went on in loud sonority with, "*Ten de kat' ophthalmon erebenne nyx ekalypsen, eripe d' exopiso, apo de psychen exapysse*—Then dark night came down upon her eyes and shrouded her away in its blackness, and she fell back, backward and gasped forth her psyche—spirit. Far from off—wildly—her head she cast the gay bright garments thereof, the frontlet and coif and kerchief and woven band, and the veil that golden Aphrodite had given her on the day when Hector of the glancing helm had led her forth as his bride from the house of Eetion, after he had given her bride-gifts untold."

And in Davis Hall, Room 106, the Ethics professor and rising village capitalist, Dr. Samuel Powers Everett, was telling his young disciples that the ethical life is the only good life, the only life that pays. "*Gnothi seauton!*" he said. And then he chuckled and asked a soft, quiet, redheaded boy on the front row, named Lowe, if he believed in God. The young man raised his startled, modest glance, adjusted his tortoise shell glasses and said he did, yes, he believed in God.

"You believe then that God is all-powerful if he is God?" Professor Everett queried innocently as he broke a piece of chalk in his strong square-fingered hand.

"Yes," said young Lowe a little apprehensively, trying to be wary of the trap and deadfall of this man, for he knew his campus reputation for deep and devious logic. But then who could be ridiculed for believing in God. And if God was God, then by definition he was perfect and therefore all-powerful. So Lowe relaxed and sat back and waited for the next finger punch below the belt.

"You see," said the professor, and his blue eyes with all their David Harum craftiness hid far away in them looked benignly out at the roomful of students. "So you see," he said, "Mr. Lowe says he believes God is all-powerful. How about you, Mr. Erwin?" And Professor Everett touched a snow-white handkerchief along the edges of his trim military-cut mustache.

"I certainly do," said the young man. And then he thought, and then agreed with himself inside that it was true. "Yes," he said, "God is all-powerful." The professor chuckled, the class looked expectantly out. "Well," said Professor Everett grinning, "we all seem to be orthodox Christians this morning. That augurs well for the salvation of the world. Excuse me a moment while I close the window. And will you close that one, too, Mr. Feldman?" Several students sprang to close the windows, but Feldman was spasmodically first. "Quite a display of grief out there this morning," Professor Everett said. "They too are calling on their God. It is a universal subject—yes. Well, this quietness is more conducive to thought"; and he went on with a chuckle, "The increased gloom also. Our windows need attention badly. Quite likely the washer is still celebrating our last week's athletic victory." And then he fired his question into the air—"You say you believe God is all-powerful, Mr. Lowe. Do you believe the Deity could cook breakfast with a snowball?"

The class sat for a moment in hushed delight. Ah, Dr. Everett! What a one he was for standing you on your head! Of course God couldn't. The snowball would melt. Then the babel of argument began, the pros and cons, the question of laws of nature, whether God could disrupt these laws, whether they were stronger than he was, and so on and so on. Professor Everett took his seat, sat back and presided easily and happily over the ferment of young minds and the vociferousness of tongues. And redheaded

Lowe sat bent and silent, aflame with a mixture of embarrassment and admiration. This, according to Dr. Everett, was the Great Process, the Hegelian Dialectic, the *Aufgehoben* of the growing soul. This was getting educated, being prepared for life.

And up in the sky-lighted room of Morehead Medical Hall, the Anatomy Class under the instruction of young Dr. Robert Lee Lauder was busy dissecting away on the great sprawled and rigid ruined cadaver of Rudolph the Negro murderer. For as the University catalogue declared — "The body is studied by systems. First the bones, then the muscles, and finally the central nervous system itself. And the student does much of the dissecting experimentally." During the entire scholastic year Rudolph and Rudolph alone had furnished himself as the sole specimen and means of study for the anatomy students. Executions had been rare in the state recently, nor had any beggars died homeless and unknown along the public highways to be picked up and carted away. For prices had been rather good, both of farm and textiles as well as heavy industry, and consequently crime and misery had lessened. Professor Lauder, the instructor, stared through the window and down toward the cemetery in the distance where the collection of Negroes were officiating at a burial. A regretful look was in his face that the dead person was being buried yonder in the ground rather than furnished here where he was so badly needed — to help further the understanding of anatomical facts and the necessary art of healing.

He moved back into the room. "We turn our attention now," he said, "to the cerebral hemispheres. In the case of Rudolph you will notice how extraordinarily large they are, though as those of you familiar with his story may know, that fact did him little good." And smiling ironically with his fine clear gray eyes, he proceeded to the serious business of the lecture.

And in Graham Hall Professor Allison Haywood was holding his class, Pedagogy 73, the same being The Curriculum, Its Principles and Practices. "One of the basic difficulties in building a proper curriculum for the teacher," he was saying, "arises from the fact that there seems to be a difference between the subjects of study which are culturally broadening and those which are practical in their benefit. There seems to be a battle going on between, for example, the humanities in university life and the vocational and technical disciplines. As, well you might say, a devotee of both, I feel the dilemma in a rather personal way. Excuse me a moment." He rose, moved across the room, and raised the window higher. He stood a moment listening to the music coming from the cemetery. The students watched him and smiled. They knew his weakness. He was caught in the pull of the singing and his avocation as student of Negro and folk mores. "I've decided to let you young gentlemen go somewhat early today," he said a little shamefacedly.

And with that he gathered up his papers and hurried from the room. The young men clattered down the stairs like a gang of heavy-footed goats, but Professor Haywood had already got his hat and notebook and was ahead of them on his way to the graveyard.

And in the cemetery the tall mother stood as before, her eyes dry as whip sockets. But the two old grandparents of the youth kept weeping softly and unashamedly away, as did some of the tender-hearted neighbors. The singing had stopped now and the old Negro preacher, pastor of the church where the boy and mother were members, was reading gently and consolingly from the open Bible in his hand. "Blessed are they that mourn," he read, "for they shall be comforted. Blessed are the meek, for they shall inherit the earth." The gentle words broke sweetly in the soft still air. "Let your light so shine before men that they may see your good works and glorify your father which is in heaven."

The mother had heard the Sermon on the Mount many a time before. But the words now read again and here on the occasion of her great tragedy brought her a vague but authoritative comfort. They had an even more holy sound here in the midst of her grief than ever they had before. It was almost as if a kindly and familiar hand had touched her or even a sheltering and protecting arm had reached around her. The tight black-gloved hands began to relax, and presently she pushed her wadded handkerchief against her mouth and closed her eyes. The melt of moisture was beginning to form beneath her lashes.

The old preacher closed his Bible and spoke gently. "Our young brother was cut off in the full promise of his prime," he said. "The cold wind of death has nipped the bud of his young days. And even as it is writ, he that goes down to the grave, shall come up no more and thou shalt seek me in the morning but I shall not be. But even say so, I know that my Redeemer liveth and that I shall stand at the latter day upon the earth. And though after my skin, worms destroy my body to pieces, yet in my flesh shall I see God. Let us pray."

All but the mother bowed their heads. Her eyes were still closed. "Our Heavenly Father," he prayed, "we know that we are nothing. As a flower soon cut down or as a wind what comes and is gone and known no more, we are nothing. Thou art all. Thy ways are mysterious and past our feeble understanding and we can only trust and believe in thee. And oh, Father, teach us faith. Teach us to be humble and accept the good and the bad alike, the dark days and the bright days, the sunshine and the rain. For as we love thee, thou certainly lovest us. And in thy love thou canst do us no evil. And I most especially pray thy comfort on this grieving mother. Let her see that all is for a purpose. And that her boy was needed in Paradise else thou wouldst not have sent for him. Teach us patience, acceptance of thy will. Even as she has lost a son, yea the more surely she shall find her eternal father. We ask it all in the name of our sweet Lord and Saviour, Jesus Christ. Amen."

"Amen," said the mourners.

And then the scene was energized to action. The coffin was let swiftly down into the grave, the boards were crossed over it and the digging shovels began to pile the dirt rapidly in.

"Ashes to ashes and dust to dust," intoned the preacher as the first thr-r-ump sounded.

The old plowman led forth in a hymn now, and the people joined richly and sonorously in. The shovels kept vying with one another as the song went on.

"Well King Jesus said, said 'Gimme some rest,
Some rest from earthly trile,'
And the words come back from the father's throne—
'A little while, in a little while.'
Then blow the trumpet and shout the praise,
And ring the bells of heaven roun'—
Old death gonna be my folding bed,
Lie down, lie down!"

The mother opened her eyes. The grave was filled and being roached up now by the patting shovels. The pine headboard and footboard were put in place. A few of the neighbors came forward with handfuls of redbud sprays, golden bell and winter jessamine and a few broken branches of sweet breath of spring which they laid on the mound. The mother saw Professor Haywood behind the group around the grave. He had arrived just before the song began. Her boy would have been pleased to know that the great Dr. Haywood had come in honor of his funeral. He had read one of Dr. Haywood's books he'd borrowed from a Negro teacher and thought it was wonderful. It told all about what the Negro in the South must do to raise himself. The water in her eyes formed a little faster. She wiped it away with her handkerchief. The song went on, and then as some of the group shifted about she saw Dr. Haywood more plainly. He was standing with one foot on a low tombstone and had a small notebook half hidden in his hand, and he was writing in it. She knew he was copying down the words of the song. He was always like that, collecting knowledge—learning, learning.

The song ended, the funeral was over, and the neighbors began to drift away. Most of them had jobs around in the community as cooks, yard men or cleaners by the odd hour, and they had to get back to their work.

Dr. Haywood slid his notebook into his pocket and came toward the mother. He had his hat off now in respect to her and the occasion.

"I'm sorry—sorry to see this, Mary Lou," he said. She nodded. "It was, it was—" he went on a little haltingly.

"Her son, Tom," said Grandma. "He was nineteen."

"Tom!" he said shocked. "I hadn't heard of it, Mary Lou."

"Yessuh," said Grandpa, wiping his old red-rimmed eyes, "Tom it was. I named him when a baby. He was a good worker." The two old people were eager, voluble before the impressive professor.

"Yes, a good worker," murmured Professor Haywood. He turned and looked heavily at the flower spread grave. "Last winter he raked the leaves out of my yard."

"He ketched his death up there at Davis Hall a week ago—that cold day, suh," said Grandpa.

"He was washing the windows and a chill struck him," said Grandma.

"Bad, too bad," said Professor Haywood grievingly. Then his voice rose irritated, a touch of anger in it. "Why didn't he take better care of himself. He should have! Yes. Why didn't he!"

"Yessuh," said the grandmother, "but he was working to save up his money, suh."

The gaunt tearless eyes of the mother looked over at Dr. Haywood. "He was planning to go up north this fall," she said, "where he could start to college."

Dr. Haywood was silent a moment. He stared at the ground, then turned aside and put on his hat. But he didn't go away. He stood there. Presently he said, "I hope you'll let me know if I can help you in any way, Mary Lou—I'll speak to Mrs. Haywood. Perhaps she'd have some extra work for you—or something. I'll speak to her."

"Thank you, sir," she said.

A moment more Professor Haywood stood there. Then he went off across the cemetery, his steps quickening as he walked. He touched the notebook in his pocket. The new song he'd copied was a real find. It would just fit into chapter five of his new book on the Cultural Backgrounds of the Southern Negro. But strangely, that fact brought him no elation. He mounted the front steps of Graham Hall, then looked back toward the cemetery. The place was deserted now except for the dark straight figure of the mother who still stood by the grave in wordless communion with her son. He went on into the building. The bell was already ringing for the next class.

For the first few minutes the lecture on Mental Tests as Necessary Aids to Social Guidance went rather lamely, as if something were bothering Professor Haywood. But then as he warmed up to his subject he became his old dynamic self again and went breezily along.

PHILLIP SHABAZZ

Letter to Paul Green

I sometimes get things wrong to get things right. — Seal

Dear Paul, this morning I opened my eyes and there was
dawn's light peeping in the window as if the sun knew
I needed her more than she needed me in these end days of June.
For me, she's the light of thankfulness. And so, I write
to you in her light since I never got a chance to shake your hand,
meet, or talk with you concerning what you will read in this letter.
I prefer to sit with you at a café in Chapel Hill and chat over tea,
but can't now that you've passed away into the gift
of her light that shines forever.

I read your story "Education South" a few days ago, and your
words see-sawed the white space and were downright arresting.
I flashed back to something you said in it, *the young white men,*
the keepers of tomorrow and the burgeoning South, were being
trained in the way they should go . . . which I took to mean
(what you did not say) trained to uphold white supremacy
and the scourge of the Lost Cause crawling through their veins,
and they were also trained to suppress Blacks. And they did. For I find
no peace or nonviolence in the rebel yell that is Confederate heritage.

I took to heart the wail of a funeral song unfolding your story,
a song that bothered the butterflies, or darkened a bowed head
at the gravesite, one long-winded sorrow song arrowing straight through
the campus and white college kids nodding over their books,

where a young Black man's life was being laid in the ground.
Yes, it was a time for mourners to sing, but for others, a time to be silent.
If that appointed hour consumed the lost minutes, and pressed
into the besieged body, no smile, no laughter, at least his burial
was with a song pushing through the dead air of human indifference.

The end becomes a journey.

After your story, and after this letter, the funeral song still rises
off the page to where *nobody loves me, but my mother,*
and she could be jiving me too. Yes, Paul, the song settles
in another song, then another, in which its blues handles
each personal tragedy, each slammed door, and faces it with grace,
lifting grief out of the gut, while its airborne glow
backs up the melody to its deepest delight, and a shirt hangs
clean on the clothesline, or a boy swims across the river,
even as the mother tree loses more leaves in November, in a season
that won't let her bear more fruit or give more shade.
This is the soul of everyday blues. All service and silence
glow from that spring. I hear the song slip up and down
the airwaves in a call-and-response chant, field holler, ring shout.
Blues voices sing the stories slanted from home talk
of the mother tongue. The sound comes to its senses in my ear
and takes me to a land beyond heartbreak, fallout, and the grave.
That soil remains a sunlit road where
such song does no harm and roses bloom on a bush
offering its rain blossoms like handwritten letters.

Light darkens the dark.

The dead young Black man in your story was my son in a previous life.
He had walked in the darkest spots of Carolina, from slum
to dope den, from a smoked-up room to youth lockup.
I'd lost him to that world, a father without his son, a void, a sign
of the times. He was wayward, talkative, and people listened.

His grin could charm a place, but he was distant as a cloud
on the night he died.

As for washing his dead body, my hands shrank.
I was so heavy with shadows, a wall of blank paper breathed
over his face gone gray. I pulled back the sheet to scrub everything
worn and dirty. Covered his private parts with a cloth.
Shut his eyes. Closed his mouth. Brushed his hair. I used a soapy
sponge to clean his flesh. I rolled him, turned him, and added camphor
to the bucket of water and rinsed his skin. Silence tiptoed around the bed.
I didn't want to hear the sorrow of a funeral song
over his body, over his soul out of body, invisible.

I couldn't see it, and I wanted to, but he cut me off.
He fell up into the stars, distancing himself from my grief
as I wiped his back and shoulders with a towel. His toes were cold.
His knee where a scar lay jagged as a weed, stiffened a little
like me, as though I were him, hounded by cannibals
for running the streets, wild, callous, hounded for chasing money
where a fired gun does not spare a dealer in the midst.

Through darkness, I dressed him for the funeral,
placed his arms alongside his body. Straightened his legs
while the drip from a faucet sent me into orbit
before reaching his final resting place. My head, my eyes
began to wander away from the shirt, the suit, the shroud.
I unlocked the door, hoisted his dead weight on my back
and carried it there, across ridges, sandhills, valleys,
a father without his son.
In All My Carolina Dreams

Part of me fled to a foxhole. Part of me hid in a mountain.
I led the life of an outcast haunted by my dead son,
until my own books, and lamps, my own table, and chair
were lost to me, even in this letter, uneasy now, bitter then,

and in that nausea, I wore the same heavy white coat.
I don't remember where I got it, which I can't stand to admit.
This was the trouble when I slept in an abandoned house,
letting its dampness lick the tremble of my lip, or vent war
on a sunflower, while I sucked its seed on my tongue.
When I covered the walls with pictures of my son's Black face,
I knew anything could happen.

Why do I tell you all this? It is because our paths crossed,
and I would not have trusted the funeral song, except,
I sing all the time. I bury sons all the time.
I hear a crowd of mourners singing in a cemetery,
while college kids withdraw to babbling professors who
still *train them in the way they should go*
like the shriek of a train ripping the track,
its wheels careening downhill through Carolina.
I see the same unconcern in a blizzard
or a hurricane spinning across the Atlantic.

As for your story finding me by that window, and my blank
sheet of paper, I wasn't sure how to call for the young dead man,
how to act as a go-between with death
so I could call him by his birth name, open my hand,
pick up the pen and leap word after black word
into the white space of this page, with grace,
that I might find a chance of light where it had been lost.

Paul Green, an undergraduate on the
University of North Carolina campus in
the fall of 1919. Photo courtesy of the
Paul Green Foundation.

The Limits of the White Gaze
in Paul Green's One-Act *White Dresses*

A late winter afternoon is over the fields, and across the land to
the West, a murky cloud creeps up the sky, lighted along its edge
by a bluish tinge from the hidden sun. . . .

   Two old sibyl-like Negro women come in from the right, one
carrying a hoe and the other a tow sack, and both creatures,
sexual and fertile, with round moist roving eyes and jowled faces
smooth and hairless as a baby's. The mark of ancient strength and
procreation still remains in their protuberant breasts and bulging
hips. Under old coats their broad shoulders and arms are muscled
like men's.—Green, *The House of Connelly* (10)

As an actress, the opening of Paul Green's play *The House of Connelly*,
makes my skin crawl. These two beautiful elders of African de-
scent, who will become a central part of Paul Green's drama,
are described in terms that feel marginalized, animalistic, and
exoticized. This reaction is a feeling that is familiar to me with most of Paul
Green's work.

   I understand intellectually that Paul Green was writing at a time when
white playwrights were not making many attempts to dramatize African
American characters as complex human beings. I understand that he was
a champion of civil rights and a staunch anti–death penalty advocate. I
admire him for these views, and I share some of them with him. I know
that the novelist Richard Wright specifically chose Green to adapt his novel

Native Son into a play after seeing a production of Green's play *Hymn to a Rising Sun*. In his day, Green was praised for his sympathetic and realistic portrayal of African American characters. I consider these traits when asked by Paul Green enthusiasts to participate in one of his plays as an actor or to direct one for staging and production. I find myself wrestling with the question, is there any value for the American theater to produce one of his plays in 2024? Why do we need to portray African American characters through the limited lens (however well-meaning it was) of a white male perspective?

Many plays by Green's contemporaries are still produced today. I was recently cast in Thornton Wilder's *The Skin of Our Teeth*. This play, originally produced in 1942, has three African American characters in the original script. One is a chair pusher in Atlantic City, the other two are a maid and a wardrobe mistress. None of Wilder's dialogue is written in dialect. No one is described in terms of skin tone or physical characteristics.

I was cast as Mrs. Antrobus, the matriarch of the family; my husband was played by a white actor. Both of our children were played by African American actors. The chair pusher was reimagined as a West Indian immigrant, in keeping with the textual exploration of an outsider in Atlantic City. Thus, by the casting, the play was moved from 1940s white America to a 2022 America. Very little text was changed.

Most white playwrights of the '30s, '40s, and '50s included characters of color as peripheral additions to the plot. They did not invest in emotional truth or depth. Green, on the other hand, made a great effort to write truthful characters of color. He used the stage to address serious social issues, writing his "negro plays" to influence understanding and sympathy for the African American community. He was also aware of his own limitations, as illustrated in his author's note to *Lonesome Road: Six Plays for the Negro Theatre*:

> In the following pages a first effort is made to say something of what these people more recently have suffered and thought and done. For it seems apparent now that such things are worthy of record. Doubtless, readers of these plays will object that they are not generally representative of the Negro race. They are not meant to be. Specifically, the chief

concern here is with the more tragic and uneasy side of Negro life as it has exhibited itself to my notice through a number of years on or near a single farm on that coastal land. Those in search of happier and more cheerful records may find them elsewhere. (xx)

I have asked myself why am I so reticent to unearth Paul Green's work for a contemporary audience? I read the one-act drama *White Dresses* (1923) to examine the cost for an actor of color to embody these well-meaning but extremely limited African American characters for today's audience.

While Green had good intentions, in most of his dramas he describes his Black characters with stereotypical references. Wide flat noses, large-boned, masculine women. The skin tone is nearly always a major factor. I realize he had many personal relationships with the men and women who worked on his farm, but despite that, he leans into familiar racist tropes. When we revisit these plays today, no director would consider following these guidelines. I don't think Green would at all be offended by that either. These descriptions reflect his era and his limited understanding of our culture. I suppose he thought he was honoring the culture. Maybe he felt he was presenting truthful depictions of men and women he had met. I don't know. Whatever his reasoning, a contemporary production can ignore those tropes and cast as needed for the story. When colorism is a theme, the range of skin tones among African American people leaves wide room for interpretation.

Next, I examine the language in the plays. Many playwrights from this period wrote in dialect. I find no shame or embarrassment in the dialect. This was the way people sounded, the playwright's attempt to capture a true voice for the characters. Green, in an effort to truthfully portray the language in the community, wrote many of his Black characters' lines in dialect. To be fair, he was not the only playwright of his era doing so. Black playwrights, including Langston Hughes, Eulalie Spence, and Mary P. Burrill, wrote characters in dialect. I do not have an issue with characters who speak in vernacular. One day, our contemporaries will likely be judged for the same thing. In one hundred years, imagine the reaction to the lyrics in *Hamilton* or the language in Suzan-Lori Parks and Ntozake Shange texts.

If one is producing one of these plays for a contemporary audience, you can approach it as you would any other dialect. There is always the option to lighten the dialect but stay true to the rhythm of the text. Green's dialect feels exaggerated to my ear, it sounds like mimicry and less like the true language of the culture.

In a production, these issues can be dealt with. Estates can grant permission to adapt dialogue and change casting. For me, the larger problem is with Green's plot and the themes. In *White Dresses*, for example, Green addresses the issue of miscegenation — sexual relationships or reproduction between people of different ethnic groups, especially when one of them is white. *White Dresses* explores love and miscegenation. It concerns an interracial relationship between a white man, Hugh Morgan, and a mulatto woman, Mary McLean. Hugh has gifted Mary with a white dress. They are in love, but Hugh's father, Henry Morgan, does not approve. Henry forces Mary to accept a marriage proposal from another man, Jim Mathews, or he will evict Mary and her elderly grandmother from their home. This makes Jim very happy, but Mary wants to reject him. In the climax of the play the grandmother reveals a second white dress to Mary, yellowed with age, making clear Henry is Mary's father — and therefore that Mary is Hugh's sister. In the last moments of the play, as Mary is trying to accept marrying Jim, her grandmother demands Hugh's gift from her. She burns both white dresses in the fireplace and says, "Dis night I's gwine wipe out some o'de traces o' sin. . . . And when dey comes to-morrow with the license, you go on and marry and you'll live respectable. . . . I knows your feelings, child, but you's got to smother 'em in" (307).

I imagine when this play was written in 1923, the idea of openly dramatizing sexual relations between Black women and white men was shocking. I imagine Green wanted to push society into a conversation on the subject. I am sure, to the first audiences, the ending was shocking — the realization that Mary's father was also her lover Hugh's father. What is the lesson in the play? Is the love between Blacks and whites dangerous because you might be related? Who is to be held responsible for the secret?

Paul Green reading before the fire in his cabin behind the family's first Chapel Hill residence, built in 1925 in The Glen. Photo courtesy of the Paul Green Foundation.

For the contemporary audience, the grandmother's revelation comes as no surprise. Black women were regularly assaulted by white men. This is one of the most damaging aspects of white supremacy. It is hard to understand how Mary would not even consider the possibility of a kinship with Hugh. Still, the fact that her grandmother holds on to this vital piece of information does not quite make sense. The end of the play allows both white male characters off without taking any responsibility. The tragedy is to be borne by the Black characters. There is no consequence for the white patriarchy. Mary is left to simply bear her loss silently.

This drama upholds the racist trope of the tragic mulatto, doomed to death and destruction, the result of the "mixing of racial bloodlines." The mulatto woman is penalized and most often dies a tragic death, proving the white supremacist view of the dangers of interracial relationships. When producing plays in the present day, one must ask why it is important that this story is told at this time. What benefit are we bringing to the conversation around race, gender, equality, diversity, and inclusion by producing a play such as *White Dresses?* For a theater practitioner, the development and portrayal of a character on stage often involves mining the character's psychological aspects, to ask an actor to embody the suffocation of one's own emotional life. Mary's grandmother tells her at the end of the play to just smother her feelings, without a critical examination of the factors surrounding the love affair between Mary and Hugh, which seems counterproductive and unimportant in today's world.

Another point in Green's plot that I find troublesome is the character of Jim. Jim comes into the play with a guitar, eager to court Mary. Mary seems to reject Jim, not only because she's in love with Hugh, but also because, as she describes him, he is "too black." Jim absorbs this criticism without any response. When Hugh's father enters the scene, Jim verbally disappears from the play. While he remains present in the room, he has very little response to the insults and the threats that Hugh's father heaps on Mary. I imagine that Green felt he was dramatizing a critical issue in the Black community. However, for contemporary audiences, the erasure of Jim as a Black man and as a human being is unacceptable. I'm not sure I understand what Green was attempting to do by silencing Jim in the room. He does not allow Jim to stand up and defend Mary. He does not allow Jim to question Mary about her colorism. And if he is using Jim as an example of the weight of white oppression, then he lets Hugh's father escape without any consequences.

Paul Green was likely attempting to use the theater to highlight and expose the inequality rural Black families suffered under white landowners. And I agree that the theater is a powerful vehicle for exposing truth and creating conversation around difficult topics. I think Paul Green was limited in his understanding of how African Americans pursued tactics to fight back against the overwhelming white oppression in our daily lives. I think he may not have understood that a grandmother, upon seeing her granddaughter in a relationship with her brother, would have warned the granddaughter much earlier. I think he may not have understood that women take care of each other. There would likely have been countless small steps and ways that a grandmother who loved her granddaughter would not have allowed the situation to progress so far. As an actor playing the grandmother, you would ask yourself that question: *Why didn't I tell my granddaughter that she was embarking on a relationship with her brother?* It's no secret in the Black community that white men regularly assaulted Black women, and many children were born as a result of those sexual assaults. Since our families were forced into separation during enslavement days, the question in the Black community "Who your people?" was asked not only to find reconnections, but also to identify familial relations. Paul Green, as a playwright, offers no explanation for the actor portraying the grandmother as to why she made this choice. He just lets her live in the world of stereotype.

For contemporary audiences and theater artists Green's plays do not invite difficult conversation. They instead dramatize the powerlessness of the African American characters in the face of white oppression. The African American characters consistently accept the limitations in their lives, the oppression in their lives, and the understanding that white society will get away with mistreating them. That is not a message I am interested in dramatizing as a theater artist. That is not a character that I am willing to embody as a Black theater artist.

When I teach African American theater history, I will often include Paul Green's work in my lectures. I understand he has an important role in the development of African American theater in the United States. I acknowledge that he fulfilled an important role in the early twentieth century by attempting to write Black characters with empathy and understanding. I appreciate him bringing his personal interactions and experiences with the Black men and women of eastern North Carolina, whom he had enduring friendships with, into his dramas. I appreciate his efforts to write these characters in an authentic voice. I acknowledge his efforts to use theater as a means of social change. With his plays he wanted America to look at the consequences of racism, poverty, and inequality. As a theater student I find all of that very interesting; however, as a theater practitioner, I find it distasteful and in many ways demeaning to embody his characters today.

Perhaps there's a world in which his plays could be produced and paired with a contemporary response by a contemporary playwright. I don't know that they could be adapted because you'd really have to change a great deal of the plots, and I'm not sure that's fair to what Paul Green was trying to do at the time that he was writing the plays. I find the plays interesting from a historical point of view but not from a production point of view. This is why I talk about Paul Green's work in my African American theater class and compare it with the works of playwrights Mary P. Burrill, Eulalie Spence, and Angelina Weld Grimké. These three African American playwrights were writing plays at the same time as Paul Green. Some of their plays were written in dialect. Some of them addressed miscegenation. Most of their plays were not produced commercially. But if I'm going to revive a play from the early twentieth century with African American characters, I'm going to do works written by one of these three playwrights. The characters they created are men and women who dramatize the fight for equality in the face of violence, degradation, and death. These African American playwrights of Paul Green's era wrote about the variety of African American characters in the community. They truthfully demonstrated the conversations that took place behind closed doors and away from the prying eyes of the white gaze.

As a theater artist it's more important for me to uplift those voices that are unsung, little known, and left behind in the theater world of the early twentieth century. For myself and for my students, it is vital that they are made aware that Paul Green was not the only playwright attempting to uplift African American voices in the American theater. It is vital that we all understand there were African American playwrights writing about Black people and white people in this same era and, not surprisingly, their voices were not commercially produced or supported. Let's lift those voices up and produce those plays. I think Paul Green would rather like that.

Comfortable and Uncomfortable
Aspects of Paul Green's *The House of Connelly* and *In Abraham's Bosom*

Paul Green is known these days as the author of *The Lost Colony*, and his identification with that pageant of North Carolina history has become his legacy to such a degree that his work as a traditional playwright—an indoor playwright, if you will—has been obscured. His essays show him to be a writer of large ambitions, connected with the finest artists of his day, winner of the 1927 Pulitzer Prize for his play *In Abraham's Bosom*, a collaborator with the likes of Richard Wright and Kurt Weill, acquainted with Eugene O'Neill and Bertolt Brecht.

Green was a theorist who demanded of theater that it be large, grand, significant, and transformative. His passion for a truly compelling theater led him to create the form he called "symphonic drama," in which music, folktale, dance, heightened language, and dramatic incident united to comprise an extraordinary artistic whole. He sought in his work to shake his audience, to challenge the norms of theater experience, and in his search for the means to achieve these goals he traveled widely, finding kindred artists in Germany and Japan, declaring Kabuki to be the greatest national theater of his experience, and seeking in his outdoor dramas to capture that greatness for himself and for his country. He had a romantic bent, always yearning. Having grown up where he did, his yearning is understandable. There is something in the flatness, the bleakness of eastern North Carolina that shapes a creative hunger in an earnest soul.

It was not enough for him to write plays; he saw himself as something larger, as someone whose art could transform others, and he strove for that greatness in every way. But at the same time, he was a child of his era and of his region, which in his case means he was the heir to the aftermath of slavery and the fact of racism, and he confronted these parts of his world with a directness that is, in retrospect, extraordinary. He believed that art—that his art in particular—could change the ugly facts of these parts of his world. He had that kind of directness that could not see a wrong without speaking of it, and he likely paid a price for that. His plays on the subject of race are all but forgotten.

Given the quality of his writing and his extraordinary sense of drama, it would be easy to decry this neglect and to declare him to be unjustly lost, but a reading of two of his most important traditional plays, *In Abraham's Bosom* (1926) and *The House of Connelly* (1931), underscores the difficulty there would be in reviving interest in Green's body of work. The plays are powerful, visceral, and moving, but they are also anachronistic in their presentation of race issues—and, for a modern audience, they veer into uneasy territory.

Is Paul Green writing a story that belongs to him in creating the saga of Abe, the mixed-race hero of *In Abraham's Bosom* who murders his white half brother in a spasm of rage? Or in *The House of Connelly*, the somber tale of the downfall or rebirth (pick your ending here) of an old southern family of self-styled aristocrats? Ownership of particular stories has become a flash point in our third-millennium world. During his lifetime Green would most likely say that of course these stories belong to him, to his southern culture, and that his upbringing in eastern North Carolina among the African Americans, poor white people, and faded gentry of his childhood entitles him to this material. A viewing of the question through a modern lens might differ with this claim. Current ideas about who should tell which story—and who should not—are more stringent than they were in Green's time, a shift brought about precisely by the comfort with which white male writers have told stories about whatever and whoever they wish, within a publishing and producing system that limited access of other voices to any kind of representation.

Green's artistry is without question in both plays, which are lyrical and powerful and operate at the highest levels of drama. *In Abraham's Bosom* is a searing, haunting experience of Jim Crow, of lynching, and of injustice.

The story of Abraham McCranie's efforts to become an educator of Black children, his struggle with his anger at the claustrophobic system of race restrictions constantly imposed on him, and his disappointment in the response of his own family to his vocation is an intense, unified, and successful play when viewed on the merits of its writing.

The House of Connelly is also a powerful experience, and in its debut—produced by the famous Group Theatre—it was praised as a fresh take on a familiar subject. Its core story is the decay and stagnation of a once-powerful southern family, which is the topic of much southern writing of the era, though its frank treatment of race broke new ground. Its weaving of stylized, choral elements into its turn-of-the-century plantation setting elevates its well-worn material into something heartfelt and fresh for its time. In its tragic conception it apparently frightened the Group Theatre a bit since its members persuaded Green to replace his original ending with a more hopeful one. (The story of this is told in Margaret D. Bauer's brilliant reading of the play for its republication in *The "Lost" Group Theatre Plays, Volume III*, and in *Paul Green's The House of Connelly: A Critical Edition*.)

But there are questions that arise from the plays in terms of fairness to the Black characters, the politics of their presentation, and the use that is made of their Blackness by their white creator. Does the heavy use of dialect and phonetic spelling justly represent the Black people in the play, or does it present them as inferiors to the white characters? Are the Black characters presented in their own terms, as fully drawn human beings with distinct lives and emerging from a culture in which they participate?

It is clear that the characters are presented as victims, and it is clear that they were victims of an incredible level of racism that has been justly described as apartheid. But is Green attempting to speak in their place, or is he speaking on their behalf because they cannot? Does he have the right to do either? These are the kinds of questions that would be asked of any play today, particularly one in which a white writer attempts to write with such focus on people of color.

These questions are less crucial in a reading or presentation of *The House of Connelly* because the focus of the play is the white family at its core. Its Black characters are featured prominently, a fact that would have been revolutionary at the time of the play's production when Broadway was scarcely

integrated at all, but the story Green is telling focuses on the decay of the
Connelly family. He is exposing the class structure of the South, which
in the play he reduces to the old aristocracy, represented by the Connelly
family; poor white people, represented by Patsy Tate and her family; and
formerly enslaved people and their descendants, many of whom are the
offspring of the Connelly males through various acts of miscegenation (and
likely acts of rape). African Americans are embodied in the play primarily
by the presence of Big Sis and Big Sue, two larger-than-life women who
haunt the play, observe and comment on the action, lurk in bushes and
corners, appear at necessary moments, and act as a chorus in a way that is
reminiscent of the Greek dramas that Green admired.

Big Sis and Big Sue are marked as different from the other characters by
the presentation of their speech. Green writes a strong dialect for both of
them, including substantial phonetic spelling (though markedly less heavy
than the phonetic spelling used for *In Abraham's Bosom*). Speaking to a sas-
safras root, Big Sis says, "Come out of that 'ere ground, old root. I gwine
boil you and drink your sap" (11). Big Sue in the same moment is watching
Will Connelly offstage and says, "Shoot them doves, Mr. Will Connelly!
You can't hit 'em and they feets red with blood" (11). These speeches are
good examples of the kind of English these characters speak, with dropped
sounds, pronoun and article misuse, and somewhat fractured grammar.
White people speak an English that is more (the Connellys) or less (the
Tates) standard. Black people do not. The effect created underscores the
difference between African Americans and all the other people in the play.
Their humanity is recognized, clearly, but their difference is underlined.

The dialogue of *In Abraham's Bosom* goes further in terms of phonetic
rendering. The story is focused directly on the lives of the Black family at its
center: Abraham McCranie, his aunt, his wife, his son, and their communities. Green writes passionately about his turpentine worker hero whose
dream is to found a school for Black children. For Abe, it is all too evident
that the white man has created a kind of open-air prison in which all Black
people are confined, hemmed in on all sides by what they are allowed to
do for work, by how they are allowed to behave in the presence of white
people, and by what they are allowed to know. Education is dangerous and
forbidden, and Abe's mission to create a school for Black children puts

him in danger all his life. Green being the writer that he is, none of this is simple or obvious. Abe has these large dreams for what he wants to do, but the flaw of his rage and the untamable nature of his emotions create a tragic flaw that is truly moving in the working out of the story.

The characters here are of the same social status as Big Sis and Big Sue, but the speech of Abe and his family is written with prominent use of "de," "dis," and "dose." Even reading the play on the page is a challenge; one constantly pauses to sound out the words (and the ancillary sounds that Green employs). The Black dialect used in the play does not impede this tragedy from unfolding, but its employment hangs over the play like a weight. One can imagine the actors attempting to negotiate the speeches in rehearsal.

There are some uncomfortable moments within the text in which Green struggles with a contradiction in the choice he has made. Abe is obsessed with books to a degree that makes one wonder why his speech has not changed by his reading. One would then expect Abe's language to conform more to standard English as he studies. Green represents this in the play at one point, when Abe appears to be succeeding in his efforts to teach school. In one short scene Abe speaks using standard spelling and correct grammar. This occurs during the preparation for a speech about his plans for the education of his people: "Abe continues his writing and then lays down his pencil and replenishes the fire. He returns to his chair and sits drumming absently on the table. . . . His speech is gentle and more cultivated" (106). His speech is marked by his use of the words "the," "this," and "that," along with "going" rather than "gwine." It is notable that the beginning scene direction notes that Abe is better dressed and that the family's Cape Fear cabin has been slightly improved in appearance. This is the play's glimmer of hope.

The relief for the reader is immediate, but the effect is temporary. By the end of the play, Abe has slipped back into his old habits of language. It is as if he is not capable of absorbing the change, as confirmed near the beginning of Scene 6: "His learning and pitiful efforts at cultural speech have dropped away like a worn-out garment and left him a criminal" (116).

Abe's speech degression demonstrates what Green intends by the playwright's use of heavy dialect spelling and by distinguishing his African American characters' speech from that of their white neighbors. Green's employment of dialect is part of his depiction of the plight of African Americans in the early twentieth century. Black speech sounds ignorant and uneducated and is depicted as such for the white ears of the time's white audiences. That is the purpose of the presentation's method and manner.

Contrast Green's usage with the current use of dialect spelling and word choice at work in a play like Katori Hall's *Hurt Village* (2013), a visceral drama about the closing of a housing project in Memphis. The play is filled with the rich textures of the speech of the neighborhood's people: bawdy, guttural, vivid, laced with obscenity. The dialogue is rendered exactly as it is spoken by these people, and its tones and word choices are modulated from person to person in the play so that we see their characters presented in the way that each of them speaks. *Hurt Village* is not a comfortable play; it represents the lives of these working-class African Americans completely, with both flaws and glories on display at all times. There is a feeling of full reality to the way that Hall creates her characters' speech. The dialect spellings feel necessary to the representation. The dialogue is written lovingly. It is lively speech, full of energy. The human speakers are fully realized.

Green is aware that educated Black people learn to speak and write standard English, indicating that this use of dialect is the playwright's choice. Abe notes in the play that he names his son Douglass for a reason. "I name you foh a great man, a man what stand high lak the sun" (101). The presence of the reference to Frederick Douglass casts a harsh light on Abe's own efforts to improve himself, which have borne so little fruit. He must himself feel this. He lacks the ability to educate himself solely by his own efforts. In his life, the presence of the kind of school he wants to create would have made all the difference.

So, both the lighter dialect used in *The House of Connelly* and the heavy dialect of *In Abraham's Bosom* indicate that Green is writing about his Black characters with a focus on their otherness. His sympathy for their plight does not overcome this feeling of separation between writer and character. In writing Black speech this way, Green was following the standard practice of the time. He appears to have struggled with the need for the phonetic spelling of dialect, using it moderately in *The House of Connelly* and heavily in *In Abraham's Bosom*. It is also true that as he aged and revised his works from younger days, he sometimes lightened the dialect of Black speakers.

In terms of the presentation of the characters in these works as fully drawn and inhabiting their own rich lives, the two plays also offer contrasts. In neither case can one separate Green's choices from shortcomings in the depiction.

In the case of *The House of Connelly*, Big Sis and Big Sue represent the two most fully drawn of the African American characters. Duffy is peripheral to the story, entering as a speaking character to beg food for his family and important to the drama only because of his family connection to the Connellys. He is one of the chief representations of miscegenation, a theme of the play, one of the sins of the fathers that is being visited on the sons. Yet we learn more about Duffy's own life than we do about Sis or Sue, even though they have vastly more stage time and are much more important to the story. Duffy has a family, loves his children, struggles to feed them, and depends on the Connellys because he has to. And it turns out that he is Bob Connelly's son. But in the case of Sis and Sue, we never learn anything in this detail. It is as if they have no lives of their own and exist purely as appendages to the central (white) family. Nor is their treatment in the play consistent. They are described in the character list as field hands. This would likely indicate that they work in Will Connelly's fields, since the rest of his land is let to tenants, and a positioning of this kind would explain their closeness to the family. But in the play's famous finale with its two differing endings, they appear to have become kitchen servants. The shift is explainable in terms of the story due to changes within the Connelly household, but it is not marked in any way.

Bauer's reading of the play, referenced previously, notes that the purpose of these two characters is figural; they are symbols as much as they are people, like the weird sisters of *Macbeth*. This is one possible explanation for the lack of detail in Sis and Sue. But they are recognizable members of their community, which Shakespeare's weird sisters are not. There is a convenience to the use Green makes of them; they exist to serve the play and have less importance in their own right. They are observers who point the audience in the right direction in the opening scene, a choral function.

In the scene with Uncle Bob, they are vixenish and lascivious, serving to accentuate his licentiousness. At the end of the play, they become crucial to the household and arbitrate the ending. Their decision in the original ending of the play to murder Patsy has a contrived feeling to it, which is likely one of the reasons for the revised ending in which she bends them to her will as servants and becomes mistress of the house. In this ending, in which Patsy enjoys a triumph over them, their obedience feels displaced. But neither ending is entirely satisfying because we do not know who Big Sis and Big Sue are.

In the play's opening scene, Green describes them as "huge creatures, sexual and fertile, with round moist roving eyes and jowled faces smooth and hairless as a baby's. The mark of ancient strength and procreation remains in their protuberant breasts and bulging hips." But there are earlier references to them as *"Two old sibyl-like Negro women"* (10). This is a troubling description. The notion that they are associated with sexuality and fertility as old women is difficult to reconcile. These are terms in which Black women are commonly described, a symptom of a racism that oversexualizes Black people, reducing Black women to protuberant breasts and buttocks. There is also here the implication that both women have had children, also meaning husbands or lovers, none of which is discussed by them (or anyone). These inconsistencies lead to an interesting meditation. Are they victims of the old dead patriarch, of his brother, or do they stand apart from the whole of the action as observers? In the latter case, why do they shed their observer status at the end of the play and attempt to act? For in both endings they have stopped watching the action and have chosen to intervene; in both endings they raise a challenge to Patsy. In the original ending they win, and Patsy dies; in the other, Patsy asserts her authority over them, and Sue and Sis slink back into the kitchen to obey. It appears to be true that Green never entirely resolved the question of Sue and Sis for himself or for his play. The cathartic process by which the Group Theatre insisted on a rewrite late in the rehearsal process would have confused the issue for him completely.

In Abraham's Bosom is a more straightforward play, focused on the tragedy that befalls Abe, caught between the better world that he wants to make and a world that is designed to crush him at every turn. Into this mix is

As the inaugural production of the Group Theatre, Paul Green's play *The House of Connelly* opened on Broadway in 1931 and was staged by Cheryl Crawford and Lee Strasberg, the legendary developer of Method acting. In 1934, the play was adapted for film as *Carolina*, starring Janet Gaynor, Lionel Barrymore, and Robert Young. More than eighty years later, in 2014, the play was reprised off-Broadway by The ReGroup Theatre, an ensemble that elected to present the playwright's original, more tragic ending. (Green had written a second, hopeful ending for the original production.) Pictured here are actors Claire Buckingham (Patsy), Sheila Simmons (Big Sis), and Selena S. Dukes (Big Sue). Photo by Mikiodo, courtesy of ReGroup Theatre.

inserted Abe's own flaws, particularly his deep, impulsive anger that so quickly flares into violence. He murders his half brother, Lonnie, when Lonnie denies him any support or aid for his dream of a school, even refusing to do anything about the beating Abe receives at the hands of local white men. This last injustice, piled onto a life of the same, unleashes a flood of rage in Abe, and he strikes out one last time. As a consequence for his crime, he is shot to death by the same men who beat him and broke him.

Abe is an amazing, complicated character, and Green incarnates him with the kind of passion and fire that makes for great theater. The play won the Pulitzer Prize, the highest mark of its excellence, and even today one

feels its power on the page despite the fact that it is difficult to read due
to the dialect spellings. But the play draws its power from the fact that its
main character and secondary characters are victims, and we watch the
terms of their victimization unfold grimly and inexorably. It would not
quite be true to say that the characters are more important as victims than
for any other quality of their lives or their selves, but the statement is very
nearly true. Green's aim in writing the play was to expose the cruelties of
the Jim Crow system in a white theater setting for a white theater audience.
Commendable as these motives are, they separate both the writer and the
audience from the material of the play: this is a drama about our white
cruelty to an *other* in our midst.

Green sees his Black characters in terms of their suffering and oppression, and the grim effect of this is that he creates little joy in their lives.
There is the moment when Abe loves his infant son Douglass and raises
him to God; there are a few moments of Muh Mack cavorting to the music
Douglass makes from his guitar. But the rest of the play is bleak. It appears
that the family's life circumstances have destroyed any possibility of happiness they might have. The play, subtitled *The Biography of a Negro in Seven
Scenes*, offers little idea of the ways that Black people struggled successfully
against oppression, the means by which they made real, full lives for themselves within the scope of work and movement they were allowed under
Jim Crow. The play omits any hint of the joy or vitality of Black life in the
South, which was very real, which existed under slavery and continued to
exist under Jim Crow laws. The play also omits the community in which
Abe lived and which might have modulated his tragedy.

To make this point more clearly it is illustrative to look at Katori Hall's
Hurt Village once again, as just one example of how an African American
writer represents the same kind of issues. The Hurt Village community is
made up of people who have suffered and continue to suffer in a world of
systemic racism, and they have limited possibilities of hope. But they have
life, joy, happiness that is all their own. The fact that they are victims of
racism and oppression does not define them as human beings. Their speech,
their relations with one another, the incidents of their lives—all the details
that a writer uses to create the character that an actor will inhabit—depict
a world in which embattled people nevertheless make a rich community.

They are lively, fierce, passionate; they are heroes and villains of their own stories; they are portraits of how people's inner strength does not allow hard circumstances to destroy their humanity.

It would be simple to claim that the difference between the two plays is due to Green's whiteness and his inability to depict Black characters fully, but Green himself was enamored of tragedy, as he notes in some of his essays. The white characters of *The House of Connelly* are equally grim and joyless; even in the marriage of Will and Patsy there is no sense of a happy ending, and they discuss love as a possibility more so than as a fact of their relationship. Green's aim in writing both these plays was to create a modern (for his day) tragedy of the scope and depth of the greatest plays from the past; he was a great admirer of Greek drama and sought to re-create some of its fire in his own writing. When framing his stories, and especially when ending his plays, he reached for the most tragic and dramatic of acts. *In Abraham's Bosom* ends with Abe's murder in the doorway of his own home, shot to death by a mob of poor white people. *The House of Connelly* ended, in its first incarnation on the page, with the murder of a poor white woman by two Black sisters. Green had an overwhelming focus on the suffering and tragedy, which he felt were transformative, cathartic, and real.

Nevertheless, in these plays he displays a tendency to discount the community out of which his Black characters emerge and to rely heavily on the victim status of these individuals without representing their resistance to it.

This leaves the final question posed earlier: is Green speaking for African Americans, or is he speaking on their behalf in an era in which Black voices were only rarely heard in print or on the stage? The evidence in the plays and in his essays suggests strongly that he was somewhere in the middle of this question. That his motives were good one cannot doubt when reading what he wrote about himself, about race, and about the need for change. But good motives are rarely enough. There are difficult moments in both plays that indicate Green's struggle with race, and this is underscored (and clarified, to a degree) in some of his essays.

In *The House of Connelly*, a telling set of stage directions is written in language that borrows from what would now be called racist tropes. The scene portrays the meeting of Will Connelly's tenants when he is announcing his new plans for the farm: "*Three or four ancient ebony darkies with faces wizened as aged monkeys beneath their flaring white hair stand respectfully near the table*" (53). The description of the men as "monkeys" should need no further explanation; the term is deeply troubling. Further along appears this passage: "*Some of the Negroes are middle-aged, tattered, and mournful like Duffy. And the others are younger, greasier and merrier, with bold gleaming eyes that roll in their sockets as they take in the splendor of the room*" (53). Again, the uncomfortable moments here are quite apparent and speak for themselves. These are, in their essence, racist descriptions, written in the author's voice in his stage directions, and they echo the earlier passage about Big Sis and Big Sue. Green is describing poor Black people as he knew them in his childhood, and his words reveal the way he sees and remembers them.

In Abraham's Bosom contains a disturbing parallel moment during the scene in which Abe's grammar has improved and when he is speaking from his heart about the issue of education:

> I been accused of wanting to make the Negro the equal of the white man. Been run from pillar to post, living in poverty because of that belief. But it is false. I never preached that doctrine. I don't say that the colored ought to be made equal to the white in society, now. We are not ready for it yet. But I do say that we have equal rights to educating and free thought and living our lives. With that all the rest will come. (110)

This particular speech feels as though it comes more from Green than from Abe, and its message is to placate the play's white audience—for the audience would have been white. It was easy for white people to decry the treatment of Blacks in the South; it was another matter to think of Black people as equals. This was the same issue that plagued the antislavery movement and the Union troops who fought the Civil War. They were opposed to slavery, but most were convinced of Black inferiority. An end to slavery or Jim Crow did not mean equality for Black people. Which begs the question of what exactly it did mean—a question that our society has never answered.

It is incorrect to equate these moments of writing with Green's attitudes toward race; both citations are small moments in large dramas. In his essay "Challenge to Citizenship," Green devotes a section to the problem of class and race in the South and notes the intertwining of the two subjects in the social structure. It is impossible to talk about race without talking about class, and the reverse is also true. (This means, of course, that the simplest solution is to talk about neither, which Green refuses to do, to his credit.) Even here he limits his comments to the Black people who remained in eastern North Carolina and speaks of them in terms of their victimhood, the fact that they have been robbed of their lives, left with only music as a means of expression. All this is true, or at least true-ish, but the Black communities of the South were far more complicated than he expresses in this essay.

In this essay, Green reserves his greatest condemnation for the poor white man, who

> produced pretty much nothing through those dreary years except himself . . . he walked his lightless track with stinking shirt and unshaven face and one gallus plough-handle stoop, oppressed by the world and the straitjacket of his religion. The juice and comedy of living were squeezed out of him, and he was left wizen-souled and dry-hearted as a shuck. The cramp of poverty, the clutch of ignorance, and the evil dreams of his lurid mind, gnarled him into bitterness. ("Challenge to Citizenship," 124)

This is the fairly typical early twentieth-century habit of post-aristocrats in the South, who blamed most of their problems on the regrettable ignorance of Black people and the intractable ignorance of "white trash." It was as if poor white people invented slavery and caused its problems to blossom while the aristocracy stood by helpless. This is not simply a problem in Green's writing but in much of the post-Reconstruction writing of the time.

So, we are left with a portrait of Green as a man who had liberal ideas about Black oppression but also the baggage of unrecognized racism. As we all do.

The issue of who is allowed to write certain material, particularly material that crosses cultures, remains unsettled. There appear at intervals artistic works that drive this question home, like Kathryn Stockett's *The Help* (2009) or Jeanine Cummins's *American Dirt* (2018). This was hardly considered an issue by the dominant culture of Paul Green's day. It was presumed that authors, perhaps by virtue of their maleness, were possessed of the magical universality that allowed them to write whatever they wished about whomever they wished. Green, who made his early reputation as a writer of "negro plays," explored the experiences of his eastern North Carolina upbringing to satisfy the curiosity of white audiences about the lives of African Americans.

Our era is not so glib or certain on this issue, which is one of the factors that makes a revival of interest in Green's work problematic. *The House of Connelly* was revived in 2014 but has faded once again into the obscurity that is the fate of nearly all plays, and nearly all art. But at least a modern edition of the play is easily accessible. *In Abraham's Bosom* cannot be found on Amazon or other popular book sites except in the market for collectible out-of-print volumes.

Despite the failings of the plays discussed here, their obscurity is a shame. Both plays are designs for great drama. Abe McCranie's story was written to confront white audiences with the injustice that existed openly in the South, and there is no other play by a white writer (that I know of) that underscores the South's propensity for vigilantism and lynching—for Abe's murder by the white mob is certainly to be counted as a lynching. It must have been a shattering experience for its audience. *The House of Connelly*, while drawn from more typical material, openly confronts its viewers with the fact of miscegenation—a word that is largely code for the sexual assault and rape of Black women by white men. While in both plays Green does not develop his stories in terms that would be acceptable to audiences today, the value of these works, particularly if presented in historical context, is extraordinary. For whatever flaws we might see in him today, Green was showing himself to be a pioneer in these plays, and taking a grave risk with his art.

Stepping Over the Line

Paul Green's *Hymn to the Rising Sun*

Although Sam Cooke's soulful ballad "Chain Gang" was written twenty-five years after Paul Green's one act "social drama" *Hymn to the Rising Sun* (1936), you can almost hear Cooke's velvety tenor voice crooning, "That's the sound of the men / Working on the chain, ga-a-ang," under the opening text as the lights slowly rise. With "Chain Gang," Cooke was subtly starting to dip his toe into the swirling waters of civil rights activism by wrapping the reality and the romanticism of the American penal system into one song. Cooke was navigating the tenuous line a Black musician with a microphone had to walk in 1960.

Green on the other hand was pushing, perhaps even stepping over, a line that a white man with a typewriter and privilege from birth could cross in 1935. Green was no stranger to overlooking and often calling attention to that deeply entrenched gulf separating race and class in the American South of his birth. He had already won a Pulitzer some nine years earlier by straddling romanticism and realism in his acclaimed *In Abraham's Bosom*, a drama with a biracial protagonist hero seeking a better life for his fellow African Americans.

A white man from the farm fields of Harnett County, North Carolina, Green was writing about the desire for a better life for Black folk in the 1920s and '30s. Green's writing, in particular his earlier works, later coupled with his activism, prompts the question: Was he an outlier or just outspoken? I would argue, both.

In *Hymn to the Rising Sun*, Green firmly plants his flag in realism, even though numerous writers before and after him would defer to romanticizing the brutalities of prison life. For centuries, artists have wrestled with the realities and the romanticization of imprisonment in their depictions of mass incarceration, with romanticism often winning out. But more often than not, reform was the underlying goal of the work.

Aeschylus's *Prometheus Bound* is a Greek play about a Titan, Prometheus, who is imprisoned for stealing fire and giving it to humans. Much like the punishment endured by southern chain gangs, imprisonment wasn't enough for Aeschylus's captor. Zeus was sadistic. Prometheus was chained to a rock, and Zeus sent an eagle to eat the Titan's immortal liver. As if that wasn't enough, the liver regrew every night, and the eagle returned daily to perpetually torment the eternally bound Titan. Shakespeare's *The Tempest* is steeped in the concept of imprisonment. Prospero and Miranda are forced to live in exile on a remote island, where Prospero enslaves the island's only native inhabitant (Caliban) and forces Ariel to do his bidding. Van Gogh painted *The Prison Courtyard* while "imprisoned" himself, in the Saint-Paul-de-Mausole asylum in Saint Rémy.

The twentieth century gave us Johnny Cash, who made Folsom Prison synonymous with carceral blues. Elvis filmed *Jailhouse Rock* on a studio backlot in Culver City, California, but nevertheless made an indelible mark on the history of movie musicals and the romanticization of prison life. His soundtrack included not only the title track, but plaintive songs such as "I Want to Be Free" and "Treat Me Nice." Both offered simple titles and reflected the overarching themes in just about every artistic depiction of late nineteenth- and twentieth-century mass incarceration. They reflected the prevalence of chain- or road-gang imprisonment, particularly in the southern regions of the U.S. where Black Americans were the overwhelming majority in prison populations.

Douglas Blackmon, author of *Slavery by Another Name*, describes the beginnings of "industrial slavery," in which convict laborers were put to work in factories or mines rather than cotton fields. Though slaves were formally emancipated by the Thirteenth Amendment to the United States Constitution following the Civil War, after Reconstruction, white-dominated southern state legislatures passed Black Codes. This "array of interlocking laws essentially intended to criminalize black life" (Blackmon 53) restricted the economic independence of Black people and provided pretexts for jail terms. Black citizens were often unable to pay even small fees and were sentenced to labor as a result; convicts were leased to plantations, lumber camps, and mines to be used for forced labor.

Put another way, Black men and women were selectively jailed on the flimsiest grounds and then essentially sold by state officials to white businesses as unpaid laborers. This massive theft of life and labor not only served the mercenary interests of white southerners, but also served as an effective tool for intimidating and punishing Black Americans for exercising their legal rights or for striving for better living and working conditions.

Living conditions for chain-gang convicts were frequently horrific. Sanitation was practically nonexistent, and diseases and illnesses were common. This was especially true if prisoners were housed in temporary living quarters — often railroad boxcars or vehicles with cages easily transported from site to site. Prisoners frequently suffered at the hands of guards, work bosses, or overseers. In December 1882, while crossing the freezing waters of western North Carolina's Tuckaseegee River, a small transport boat carrying nineteen Black prisoners, all shackled to one another, capsized, sending the men into icy water where they drowned, unable to swim to shore. Black prison laborers were often starved to death, maimed, or beaten to death by "whipping bosses."

News of these conditions gave rise to organizations such as the Joint Committee on Prison Reform (JCPR). Moreover, the late 1910s elevated the prison reform film to a prominent place within popular culture according to historian Alison Griffiths, author of *Carceral Fantasies: Cinema and Prison in Early Twentieth-Century America*. She cites films like *The Right Way* (1921), *The Big House* (1930), and *I Am a Fugitive from a Chain Gang* (1932) as inciting the awareness and need for wide-scale prison reform. *I Am a Fugitive from a Chain Gang* garnered three Academy Award nominations. The growing popularity of these films made American audiences begin to question the legitimacy of the U.S. legal system, at least for white Americans. For all the national outcry for reform, the forced labor of Black men and women, particularly in the South, continued with little change.

The most extensive use of road and chain gangs in North Carolina paralleled the expanding growth of highway construction accompanying the Automotive Age, from 1900 to 1950. Perhaps Paul Green took note of the disparity in these popular films or was indeed outraged at the series of tragedies that continued to befall Black chain-gang laborers in North Carolina and across the South. Yet again, I would argue, both.

———

Paul Green was arguably among the first to integrate the University of North Carolina at Chapel Hill by inviting to campus nationally acclaimed Black writers such as James Weldon Johnson and Richard Wright. Green himself attended and even hosted meetings at his home in 1935 with groups of prominent social and political influencers that would today be seen as activist organizations for civil and workers' rights. By then, Green was moving between the film and theatrical worlds. His reputation as a social activist brought solicitations for help literally to his doorstep. One such request came in a phone call from a news reporter in Charlotte. An appointment was set, and the men met at Green's home. The journalist arrived with a manila envelope. During their conversation, he fished several photographs from the envelope and handed them to Green. Green incorporates the moment in his novel *This Body the Earth*: "I looked at them. There was a picture of two Negro men, each one sitting in a wheelchair and his feet bound up, on the ends of his legs. He didn't have any feet . . . and I said, 'What in the world happened?' And he said . . . 'Those two men have had their feet amputated' " (qtd. in Wynn VI-26). The reporter told Green that these men, Robert Barnes and Woodrow Wilson Shropshire, were sent to solitary confinement in a North Carolina chain-gang "dark house" in January 1935 because they warmed their feet at a roadside fire after a guard told them not to. The men were manacled upright ten hours a day for nine days with very little heat in the day and none at night. Frostbite set into their feet and gangrene thereafter. When their conditions were finally addressed, a prison surgeon amputated the men's limbs halfway to the knees. "It is astonishing," the prison physician falsely testified, "how some prisoners will mutilate themselves to escape work" (qtd. in Henderson).

In learning the story of Barnes and Shropshire, Green says, he could not resist assisting the men. Green used his prominence to move the levers of justice toward obtaining compensation for the prisoners. About this incident, he wrote, "So I go over to the governor and show him these pictures and say, 'Here is something terrible that has happened' and he said, 'Well there is nothing we can do.'" Green pressed the governor to no avail—until, Green threatened, "I know the Paramount News man in Hollywood, and when I get home I'll call him in Hollywood and tomorrow or the next day we'll have a team of photographers here and we'll photograph these boys. We'll cover the whole United States with their pictures" (Hall 52).

The governor relented, and eventually the men were pensioned. Because Green had used his influence to get the men compensated, he could no longer make good on his threats to the governor to spread the story in the national press. However, his passion and interest in prison reform did not wane; in fact, it grew.

Green began immersing himself in understanding what life as a prisoner in North Carolina was like. And that research prompted him to write a play starkly different from—and harsher than—any other he'd written. His one-act play *Hymn to the Rising Sun* challenged the sadistic treatment of prisoners, in particular African Americans, in the North Carolina penal system. The play is a continuous scene during a single morning on a convict chain gang. The prisoners are perpetually terrorized by The Captain, a white overseer type. A young white man called Bright Boy, new to the chain gang, is tortured by the wailing and weeping of Runt, a Black convict imprisoned all night in a hot box maniacally referred to as "Aggie." The Captain is a horrifying yet sometimes understated character whose authority is absolute. In the end, he horsewhips Bright Boy brutally, and Runt dies in the box. Ironically the entire play takes place on Independence Day.

Perhaps it is because it is a one-act play, with only one setting and a handful of players, that Green was able to avoid the pitfalls of romanticizing prison in the vein that so many of the pulp prison films of the time fell victim. Perhaps it was knowing the very real story of Barnes and Shropshire that gave him the solid ground and the bully pulpit to preach from. Perhaps it was the substantial research he had done. Or perhaps—and this I believe to be most true—because the play's dialogue by and large is spoken by Captain Huff, the central character and antagonist, Green avoided the pitfalls of romanticism. This white overseer-type figure strikes fear in not only the prisoners, but the guards as well. Green knows this man. He's met and spoken to Captain Huffs throughout his lifetime in the South of his birth, obeyed orders from them in the army of his youth, and railed against them in his writing as an adult. Huff's words pour from his mouth with unwavering disdain for these prisoners, like the benevolent slave master he believes himself to be. He toys with them like a sadistic sharp-toothed house cat who's too domesticated to eat the broken-winged bird and yet too barbarous to let it go. Because Green knows the arguments both for and against prison reform, he's able to successfully play both sides of the argument deftly from the perspective of Huff with Shakespearian skill.

CAPTAIN HUFF: I ain't had a chance to make you a speech since last Easter when I talked on the Resurrection. But orders from the headquarters say I must call your attention to the occasion. . . . Well boys, orders is orders, as some of you ain't never found out and I take great privilege on our Independence Day of once more addressing a few words unto you. . . . According to statute number six hundred and forty-two of the penal code duly proved and entered in the House of Representatives, so I'm told by a vote of ninety-six to four, the punishment for constant trifling and belly aching is twenty-nine blows with the whip. . . . But did I ever whip a man that much? I say did I?

PEARLY GATES: No sir.

CARELESS LOVE: No, Cap'n.

CAPTAIN HUFF: You're damn right I didn't. (192–93)

Unfortunately, Green ultimately veers off into familiar tropes and stereotypes that weaken the play's argument. At the heart of prison reform should be man's ability to see the humanity in his fellow man. What made a century of slavery possible was the use of religious dogma that engrained the myth that Black people were less than human. What made a century of segregation, white supremacy, and terrorism possible was the use of religious dogma that seemed to support the myth that Black people were less than human. And what continues to spur violence against Black and brown bodies still today by white terrorists and even some police is the ingrained myth that Black people somehow do not feel pain in the same manner as their white brethren. In *Hymn to the Rising Sun*, Green describes Black characters as being animal-like in their behaviors or features—subtly layering in a myth that undercuts the play's entire thesis. Here are some

Green entertained groups of writers often in his home, though the literary community was overwhelmingly white and male at the time. Seated from left: George Hall, Manley Wade Wellman, Betty Smith, and George Brenholz. Standing clockwise: Robert Hilliard, J. A. C. Dunn, Thomas Patterson, John S. Clayton, John Ehle, Paul Green, Thad Stem Jr., and Ralph Dennis. Photo by UNC Photo Lab, courtesy of the Paul Green Foundation.

examples from Green's stage directions: "*The Negro at the left shakes himself like a huge, chained animal*" (182) and "*The Captain stands watching them indulgently, like a circus master with his trained pets*" (188). Green also describes Black characters in ways they would have been described by their former slave masters: "*The Negroes led by Pearly Gates come out and join the end of the line. There are eight of these, four young bucks, an old bent mulatto, and three middle aged fellows*" (186).

In the modern theater these are all issues that can be fixed and should be fixed if the play is going to continue to be a bullhorn for prison reform. However, there are some tropes that are even more cumbersome to address and cannot go unchanged or unaddressed in the script. These historically problematic tropes raise the reddest of flags. With the character Runt, Green has written into his play yet another oversexualized Black man. The very reason Runt is placed in solitary confinement, we learn, is because Captain Huff accuses him of masturbating. Runt calls himself "The Bull of The Woods." Green could have found another crime for Runt to perpetrate without once more bringing a Black man's sex figuratively into full view. That is a bell that cannot be unrung in the minds of many white theater goers of that day, and perhaps even now. Green does a disservice to his entire play by leaving it in.

A final trope that Green employed and that also continues to plague white writers to this day is the "white savior." In *Hymn*, Bright Boy does his best to save Runt, making arguments and pleading his case from start to finish. I understand that Green could be making the case for white allyship, whatever the definition of that might have been in 1935. However, in *Hymn*, Green makes Captain Huff's cruelty the central voice and character. I would suggest contemplating the play from the perspective of a Black American; doing so, one might find that Runt's unanswered cries are the true central voice of the play. But because Runt is never able to make the case for himself, the audience is left with another dehumanized Black body.

In many ways I see *Hymn to the Rising Sun* as a solo performance by Captain Huff. In all his ignorant, narcissistic glory, Huff is vilely making Green's argument for prison reform by doing what all egomaniacs and demagogues do best: make speeches. If Paul Green could see how large American prisons have become, if he could see the overwhelming lack of oversight in the decades since his death, I do believe it would be his highest priority to see that *Hymn to the Rising Sun* is produced in and outside prisons around the country.

––––––

For me, this play cuts close to the bone. Some years ago, my older brother was arrested, tried, and imprisoned in a southern penitentiary. While "inside" he developed type 2 diabetes, which went unchecked, eventually leading to the amputation of three toes on his left foot and all five on his right.

Not many years after he was finally released, jobless and in poor health after paying his debt to society, he sadly succumbed to the disease, which he was never able to manage.

Each year thousands of incarcerated and formerly incarcerated Americans die from preventable health issues. According to the Vera Institute, a not-for-profit organization working to end mass incarceration in the U.S.,

People who have not been convicted of crimes are losing their lives while awaiting trial because they can't afford bail.

The United Nations Committee Against Torture has expressed concern about reports of deaths caused by extreme heat in unbearably hot and poorly ventilated prisons in Arizona, California, Florida, Michigan, New York, and Texas.

People with mental health conditions are losing their lives in prisons where symptoms of mental illness are met with brutal punishment instead of treatment.

The United States has the largest carceral system in the world and far too much of it operates in shadows. We can't solve the problem of in-custody deaths unless we can shed light on it. (Bryant)

My brother's crime in 2006 was possessing marijuana. Today, nineteen states, two territories, and the District of Columbia have legalized marijuana.

Leaning Toward the Light

There was going to be an execution.

A fifteen-year-old Black boy in western North Carolina had been charged with raping a white woman. The jury deliberated five minutes, then gave their verdict: guilty. When Paul Green heard about the boy, he went to Governor Clyde Roark Hoey, a fine church man, one who listened intently to the sermon each Sunday, even led a Bible class. Paul Green insisted that the boy was too young to be executed and asked the governor to intervene. Governor Hoey responded by reading a letter from the county sheriff about the young man: "I remember time and again walking the streets at night, or some of my men, and finding him robbing garbage cans as a boy. . . . He has been at it since he was ten years old." The governor added the damning words, "You see, Paul, he is just naturally a criminal." Imagine the impact of these words, the double slap of recognition and disbelief, before Paul Green said, "Great God, Governor, the poor boy was hungry" (Hall 49).

That double slap of recognition and disbelief has haunted much of our work at the nonprofit Hidden Voices, encouraging men and women living in prison, including many on death row, to share their stories. The notion that children are somehow born criminals, that their lives of deprivation and violence are somehow their own fault—or their family's fault—and not the actual responsibility of the rest of us who have participated in and benefitted from the system that set them up to fail—that narrative persists to this day. Yet one can only listen to so many stories of children who were hungry, abused, abandoned; children from poor communities, underresourced schools, and overpoliced communities; children bewildered by a violent and uncaring world, who learned early that the rule of life was "eat or be eaten." One can only listen to so many of these stories before wondering what the rest of us are hungry for? Could it be justice?

If we listen to those stories with curiosity rather than judgment, we can't help but land in some pretty uncomfortable territory. The stories raise the possibility that we have been misled, that what we have assumed to be true of those convicted and the system that convicted them may not be the case at all. Really, we hardly need data and statistics. A visual will suffice. Walk onto death row and look around. Once you see who's there, you cannot *not* understand.

Very few people on death row are wealthy. Few are even middle class. And there have always been far, far too many grown, or nearly grown, children of color.

Fortunately for all of us today, Paul Green had both a questioning mind and a compassionately curious nature. People say that when he listened to you, leaning slightly forward, his gaze focused and clear, you knew he was not formulating a response or doing anything but that one simple thing: listening, with his full attention and care. It was this sympathetic listening that allowed space for the important questions, the clear seeing, to arise. Green was willing to question. If an idea, a belief, a system couldn't stand up to inquiry, what use was it?

Green received a scholarship to a Baptist college but chose to earn money picking cotton and playing semipro baseball to pay his tuition at the University of North Carolina, where he would, according to the cautionary words of those around him, "lose his religion." Green was willing to chance it. If people thought differently than how he'd been reared, they must have a powerful reason, and he could likely learn something from them. That willingness to inspect one's own assumptions, one's most foundational beliefs, requires great courage or great curiosity or both. For Paul Green, it was both.

From the beginning, Green wanted his writing, his characters, and his actions to be "on the side of something that counts for others" (quoted in "Paul Green"). He was often one of the only, sometimes the only, voice raised in protest to some "damnable senseless prejudice" (Avery 136). His outspokenness and his art were the inevitable, unavoidable, outcome of a man who staked his life on the inherent dignity of the human spirit.

At a 1944 meeting of the Roanoke Island Historical Association in Raleigh, Paul Green stands behind Governor J. Melville Broughton (seated). Two years earlier, Governor Broughton pardoned William Mason Wellmon, a Black man sentenced to death for the rape of a sixty-seven-year-old white woman. Green had advocated for a stay of execution for Wellmon, based on a verifiable alibi that was missed in the original trial. Thanks to Green's advocacy, Wellmon became "the first person in the state acquitted of a crime for which he had been sentenced to death," according to Laurence Avery's account in *A Southern Life: Letters of Paul Green*, p. 442. Photo by NC News Bureau, courtesy of the Paul Green Foundation.

In a letter to a reporter and friend in the 1920s, Paul Green noted that the perspective of the great beings, including Jesus, was not limited to a particular place or time. For them, there was "neither black nor white, Jew nor Gentile—but people, people, everywhere people." That same decade, Paul Green won a Pulitzer Prize for his play *In Abraham's Bosom*, a play that the Pulitzer committee described as bringing us "face to face with one of the most serious of the social problems of this country" (Fischer 24–25). In the play, Abraham says, "ain't no difference at the bottom. . . . it's the man that counts" (65).

This recognition of our mutuality was not exactly a guiding light for legislatures or institutional leaders, who seemed only concerned, as Paul Green saw it, with profit and loss and the changeable political fortunes of those who took a stand. I think the constant caution from politicians and other leaders to "go slow, be careful, soft pedal" likely infuriated Paul Green (Avery 136). The constant admonition from those in power against being reckless and possibly ruining the meager progress being made must have seemed an affront not only to him but to the lives of those wasting away in prison, to the Durham tobacco workers being paid a quarter for every thousand sacks they strung, to the janitors and brick masons building the University of North Carolina campus who were neither paid a decent wage nor allowed to attend classes or check out books from the university's library.

Paul Green railed against it all, saying that as best he could tell, "Jesus was a most reckless person" himself. If the Jesus he knew had attended those legislative sessions that failed to restrict the KKK or to pass increased funding for education—and had been "provided with a good whip"—that Jesus would have adjourned those gatherings "sine die" (Avery 136).

In 1934, while working in Hollywood, Green learned about the Bittings case, in which a Black tenant farmer, a World War I soldier, shot a threatening and abusive landlord. Paul Green wrote, "I am not entirely against capital punishment as such, for from the true horticulturalist point of view there are evil members to be pruned out, but I am absolutely opposed to it . . . as it is carried out in North Carolina" (Avery 232–33). His telegram to the state parole commissioner sounded an even stronger note: "Any social system which provides such an array of human tragedy as we have on death row today stands condemned with the criminals themselves" (Avery 232). Almost ninety years later, those words still stun: we stand condemned.

Yet Paul Green wrote this during the 1930s, when support for the death penalty was at a peak, when criminologists argued the death penalty was a necessary social measure, when there were more executions than any other decade, and when there was no significant opposition to the death penalty. To put Green's stance in even starker context, the last public hanging in the United States of America took place *two years later*, in 1936. Hopeful viewers traveled from neighboring states in cars, trucks, and trains. Hotels were full, and according to the newspapers, concessions were erected serving beer and sandwiches. Twenty thousand people attended. It took the young man dangling at the end of the rope fifteen minutes to die. This is the backdrop against which Paul Green said, "We stand condemned." It wasn't exactly a popular view.

In a 1945 letter to Governor Cherry, Paul Green wrote even more definitively, "I am completely opposed to capital punishment as a part of our penal system" (Avery 409). His opinion about the function of a death penalty had shifted from the occasional necessary "pruning" to opposing the practice entirely. What changed his perspective?

I think it was his personal interaction with specific individuals who were experiencing the death penalty in action. From prisoners to politicians to jurors to chain-gang bosses and wardens, Paul Green was confronted with the actual face of what is for most people only a conceptual abstraction. The death penalty became a living, breathing person, with family and friends, a history, and a particular action that had landed them in a system of justice that was racially motivated and rooted in "the old Mosaic law and a perverse and pessimistic philosophy of mankind" (Avery 409). It was a living system run by fallible humans who made mistakes, even with the best of intentions, and one where good intentions were often nowhere to be found.

Paul Green once said, "There can be no sin but the denying of the spirit of man" (Avery 136). His grandson and namesake, the attorney Paul Green, shared how his grandfather, in Europe at the end of World War I, was walking through the rubble and destruction of a French village when he came upon a sort of souvenir. Unlike many young soldiers, including my own grandfather, Paul Green did not bring home a scavenged Luger or dagger or belt buckle as his battle trophy. Amidst the war debris, Paul Green uncovered a small statue of Mary with her infant child, chipped at the base but somehow still intact. What a wonder. He carried the statue across Europe and England until he finally arrived back in the United States. A few years later, he gave the statue to his fiancée as her wedding gift. Paul Green, as his grandson explained, "always looked for the good."

One cannot be involved with the justice system in even a marginal way without becoming aware that no one is looking for the good. Denial of the spirit is pervasive and intentional. The system was and is designed to dehumanize and derelationalize. This "sin" is not something confined to a few extreme cases; it is systemic. And it affects everyone involved, not just the convicted.

Green did his utmost to expand the narrative by bringing to light a more complex understanding of their context. In 1931, for example, nine Black teenagers were accused of raping two white women while riding a freight train. The boys were transferred to a jail in Scottsboro, Alabama. By the third day of their trial, eight of the nine "Scottsboro boys" had been convicted by an all-male, all-white jury and sentenced to death. The years of trial and retrials created an international uproar. Soon after the initial trial, the International Labor Defense, the legal wing of the Communist Party in the U.S., recognized the potential for the case to further their goals and so began organizing parades, rallies, and demonstrations, against the wishes of the NAACP, which was representing some of the boys.

Perhaps surprising to some, Paul Green stated in the bluntest terms that he was not interested in the cause. But he was interested in "the particular saving of these particular boys." He understood how the sacrifice of these boys, their "legal lynching," might further the cause of a socialist movement, their lives a sacrifice to the cause, and he was having none of it. In an open letter to Theodore Dreiser, he wrote, "Please, Mr. Dreiser, throw away your politics and your theories this once and pray and work with us that mercy be done! For it would be an everlasting sin for you to use the bones of seven Negro boys to hammer the drums of a social revolution" (Avery 202). Paul Green maintained in the most public way possible that there was one duty, and one duty only: to free the clearly innocent Scottsboro boys. As he wrote in a letter to John Dos Passos, "Think of it — Roy Wright 15 Eugene Williams 14 still behind the bars after 18 months! And no hope in sight! As I write these words they might be out playing cat with other boys in the alley, or tag, or helping in the fields, or fishing down at the old swimming hole — breathing the fresh air — happy boys. . . . My God what are we — men or brutes!" (Avery 210).

It was the dignity of specific human lives that motivated Paul Green, and whether he was speaking of the human cost of war or of social reformation, his attitude was: save the boys and the cause will save itself. Or, if need be, "save the boys and to hell with the cause."

In 1935, *Time* magazine published an article with the headline, "Price of Progress." Two men in North Carolina had been sentenced, for relatively minor infractions, to serve on a chain gang. The "Good Roads State" was built by convict labor. The two prisoners tried to warm themselves by a roadside fire after a guard warned them not to; as a result, the men were manacled upright ten hours a day for nine days. In other words, the men were tortured. Their feet froze and had to be amputated. The *Time* article closed by saying, "Since North Carolina public opinion is thoroughly aroused against the Negroes' keepers and the whole reeking chain-gang system, consensus was that Robert Barnes's and Woodrow Wilson Shropshire's lost legs would be the price of a new and more merciful penological system in the State" ("Price" 16). Such was this *price of progress.*

The price was unacceptable to Green, who, explaining to Governor Hoey, lay responsibility squarely in the State's lap: "Governor, these are a couple of fellows that the State of North Carolina has cut their feet off" (Hall 52). The governor agreed it was a terrible situation and expressed his regret that there was nothing the State could do about it. The State couldn't agree that it was liable or responsible since, without that acknowledgment, the men couldn't sue the State. Green kept insisting North Carolina must take care of the men. When the governor continued to refuse, Green said he supposed he'd have to do something himself. Probably relieved, Governor Hoey said, "Good luck, Paul, do what you can for them" (Hall 52).

Here's what Green offered to do: "I'll call [a Paramount newsman] in Hollywood and tomorrow or the next day, we'll have a team of photographers here and we'll photograph these boys. We'll cover the whole United States with their pictures" (Hall 52). "You can't do that," the governor protested, to which Green replied, "You are damn right I can. And I will" (Hall 53). The State pensioned the men.

The human cost of these horrifying cruelties—chain gangs and solitary confinement, sweat boxes and dark houses—moved Paul Green to write. When his play *Hymn to the Rising Sun* was published, about a prisoner's solitary confinement and death in a hot box, Green bought two hundred copies of the play himself and sent one to each newspaper editor, each representative, and each senator, along with a letter.

He never heard a word from any of them.

Abolition of the death penalty wasn't a cause célèbre for Paul Green. Unlike today, there were no online petitions to sign with a click. Challenging the death penalty meant the dogged questioning of one individual case after another: reading transcripts and documents, making lists of facts, traveling to the prisons to interview prisoners, meeting with governors and public officials. And writing—my God, how he wrote! He wrote letters to defense attorneys and prosecuting attorneys, to governors and legislators, to editors of papers. He wrote plays, stories, articles. When he wrote the attorney prosecuting William Mason Wellmon, Green listed eighteen points he considered unclear or worthy of investigation. Wellmon was clearly innocent: not only had the victim not identified him in a lineup, Wellmon had been in another state entirely at the time of the crime. Yet even with a verifiable alibi, Wellmon was held in Raleigh's Central Prison for two years before Green and others finally convinced Governor J. Melville Broughton to investigate Wellmon's innocence and eventually pardon him.

And so it went. Case after case, governor after governor, decade after decade. Paul Green understood that to mend the social fabric, to rebuild the lives of the most disenfranchised, required starting "at the bottom with education and encouragement and understanding with one another" (Avery 468, n.1). Absolutely. But the state wasn't interested in funding equal and inclusive education any more than it wanted to support citizens building bonds of solidarity and understanding. In the meantime, the death penalty was widely employed, killing the poor, the uneducated, the mentally ill, and the developmentally disabled. Paul Green acknowledged that saving a single life might not seem like much in the scheme of things, but it was the only place we had to begin.

It still is. The narrative of who is charged and convicted shifts when we connect across difference, one story at a time, one human life at a time. Paul Green was still the cotton picker, still the farm boy who needed "to work up a good sweat every day." But his understanding was growing more nuanced. He now saw human life in a context of available light. "I believe that human beings are like plants; they lean toward the light, they grow better toward the light. . . . And man tends toward the good" (qtd. in Ladd).

A few years ago, a man living on death row sent me a letter describing how two geese had taken up residence in the prison's rec yard. Of all the possible places in the world, the geese had decided the best spot to build a nest was inside a prison compound. The men soon realized the female had laid a clutch of eggs. Some of the guys, concerned about the summer heat, made a little tub to hold water. They sat it where the mother could drink without leaving the nest. When the men were allowed outside for their hour of rec, the first thing they checked was whether she needed more water. Some even sneaked out bits of bread to feed her.

On the day the shells broke open, men who hadn't ventured outside in twenty years came to see the hatchlings, "watching them stumble and bumble around their new surroundings." New life! It's easy to imagine the tiny fluffers blinking in the unfamiliar light, surrounded by men doing the exact same thing: blinking in the unfamiliar light.

Eventually Animal Control took the birds away. Everyone agreed it was best. The environment wasn't exactly conducive to healthy development. They might be easy prey for foxes, hawks, vultures—it was no place for babies to fledge. Not if they wanted to survive. Still, the day Animal Control took the geese, the men who went outside noted how the absence of life felt oppressive, the rec yard appearing "like the empty dirt lot it is. Only more so."

That hard dirt is not a soil in which much can grow, much less flourish. Yet kindness, compassion, and tenderness spring up in even the most hard-packed places. As Green reminded Governor Robert Gregg Cherry, to kill someone in "judicial cold blood is but to deny any possible development and amelioration in that man's character. This is not only bad science but worse Christianity. For you and I know that as long as there is life, there is hope for improvement" (Avery 409). Killing someone stops the story, and we have no way to foresee how that story will end.

More than once, on admission to the hospital, Green was asked for his religious affiliation. His response? "Humanist." Imagine the admitting clerk's uncertainty. "We don't have a code number for that. Can you think of something else?" He could not.

Green wrote, "I will not live to see it, but perhaps my children will—the relegation of such instruments as the electric chair, the gas chamber . . . to the museum as an inspiration to a new age and a warning to our young people as to the blindness in which a former generation walked" (Avery 409). *The blindness in which a former generation walked.* However much his generation might avert their eyes, Paul Green was willing to see. He traveled to death row where boys as young as fourteen were waiting to be executed, sometimes for burglary. It seems unbelievable now, but until the 1940s, North Carolina had a mandatory death sentence for first-degree burglary. Green would tell the prison officials, the newspaper editors, the line of governors, "You're wrong to do this." And when the officials wouldn't listen, Green would use his own money to hire lawyers. He visited the condemned, and when it came time for their killing, he stood vigil outside the prison, usually alone.

When I was working on death row, some of the men living there told

stories of those who stood outside the prison on Christmas, holding ban-
ners and singing carols, or who stood vigil during executions. One man said
that after a particularly hard Christmas Eve, when the prisoners were reel-
ing from repeated executions of their friends, he heard an older man calling
them to look out their windows. "A line of people stood outside—yelling,
waving, and holding a sign that read: *Merry Christmas*." His reaction? "Here
I was, struggling to maintain my sense of humanity, and complete strangers
that didn't even know my name were out there reminding me of it."

Who were they? Pen pals of the men, friends, family, church people.
Humanists.

Even the men who were skeptical, who felt that in the end, the protestors'
presence was like throwing money into a wishing well—an action, but one
that did no real good—could still appreciate the effort it took for people to
leave the comfort of their homes and travel to the capital, to stand out in
the cold on Christmas Day. One man questioned whether he himself would
have done the same, year after year, execution after execution.

It must have galled Green to be told over and over for so many decades
that change is slow, that "you can't do this overnight." But overnight is
exactly what he did. Execution after execution. Did his vigils outside the
penitentiary do any good? I suppose it depends on how we understand *good*.
Certainly his other efforts—the letters, plays, phone calls, visits, funding—
did real and tangible good. But planting himself outside the prison, witness
to a drama for which he could not script the end, that did a different kind of
good. The image of his "lone vigil," as it's known, stands as a challenge to
us all. It reminds us that every life has significance. And that it is we who
are each other's keepers.

Paul Green didn't just walk his talk, he bushwhacked a path for others to
tread today. His challenge remains: *while we are here, let's write a great story.*

We are still trying to write that story. Ninety years can seem like a very
long night. But even when we cannot see, much less write the end of the
story, we show up. We do not turn away. Green left us this legacy, and so
we lean toward the light and trust that the light within each of us will lead
finally toward the good.

Problems of the Hero

The Many Endings of *Native Son*

I n a hotel room in New York, in the early spring of 1941, two of the greatest writers of their generation encountered a problem they could not resolve. A problem that amounted to less than a page of dialogue but represented a rift between two views of man and our place in society. A problem that became the fatal flaw in what should have been the most successful play on Broadway that year. And, as a playwright myself, a problem that captured my imagination immediately.

The production in question was the Broadway adaptation of Richard Wright's novel *Native Son*. The novel, published the previous spring, was a blockbuster, selling a quarter of a million copies in its first three weeks. It was the most successful novel by a Black author up to that time, and it succeeded in spite of (or perhaps because of) its completely uncompromising vision of the violence and terror visited upon poor Black communities. It is a gruesome crime novel, centered on Bigger Thomas, a character Wright declared was the inevitable product of poverty and racism.

Displeased by the fact that his first book, *Uncle Tom's Children*, was "a book bankers' daughters could read and weep and feel good about," Wright determined that *Native Son* would be "so hard and deep that they would have to face it without the consolation of tears" (Wright, "How," 27). The book's success, along with that insistence on hard and deep truth, set the pattern for Black writers for a generation. As James Baldwin said, "No American Negro exists who does not have his private Bigger Thomas living in his skull" (32).

In the summer of 1940, Wright was the biggest star in American literature. Offers for a stage adaptation poured in throughout that summer, but the team Wright eventually accepted were all stars of a similar stature.

The adaptation was to be produced by Orson Welles and John Houseman's Mercury Theatre, already legendary for their radio production of *War of the Worlds*. Welles himself would miss most of the adaptation process, since he was in California filming *Citizen Kane*. But just as famous was the author chosen to write the script: North Carolina's Paul Green.

Green was the obvious choice: a Pulitzer Prize winner and America's preeminent Southern playwright, whose work Wright himself had directed in Chicago. After an initial meeting in July, Wright came away certain Green was the writer for the job. Green's agent wrote him the following week, saying, "Mr. Wright made it very clear in his talk with me that he wanted you to dramatize the book with him, and no one else and that that was of paramount importance in his mind" (Reynolds, June 25).

Wright's enthusiasm was matched by Green's as they started work on the script, but after an initial promising period of collaboration, these four titans ended up at odds with each other. Deep disagreement arose over the style, tone, and purpose of the play, as well as over its fundamental philosophy. Most of all, that disagreement focused on the final pages of the play, which were revised over and over again.

Approached by EBZB Productions to write a play about Green and his place in the American canon, I realized that what happened in the New York hotel room where Wright and Green struggled to make that ending work was the stuff of great theater itself: two brilliant men, wrestling over their deepest beliefs. A great reckoning in a little room indeed.

I was inspired by Margaret D. Bauer's excellent essay about their collaboration, "Call Me Paul: The Long, Hot Summer of Paul Green and Richard Wright." It was here that I saw that perhaps the struggle was not just about two philosophies, but also about two men, a Black genius and an established white author, trying to navigate both friendship and the artistic process.

While the play of course is a work of fiction and an imagining of what happened in that room, I wanted to make sure I only expressed ideas these men had stated elsewhere, and that I was faithful to the chain of events as they happened. This was only possible because of the work of Curtis R.

Scott. In his "How Bigger was Reborn," he meticulously re-created the timeline from the publication of *Native Son* as a novel through the play's opening on Broadway. Later accounts of that process by Paul Green and John Houseman tended to play Rashomon with the history, suggesting clear villains and heroes. But in Scott's analysis of the correspondence and diaries of the writers during that time, he revealed something much more human and more akin to the creative process I recognize: a group of people with immense respect for each other, laboring with good faith and honest determination, and still ending up on opposite sides of a great divide.

To understand that ending, however, it is necessary to understand the beginning, and by all accounts, the initial process of drafting the script went remarkably well. According to Scott's chronology, Wright arrived in Chapel Hill in early July 1940 and stayed four weeks, working with Green on the University of North Carolina campus. Green's own recollection, in an interview with Rhoda Wynn in 1974, was that he wrote most of the dialogue, turning to Wright for input and guidance, while their secretary, Ouida Campbell, remembered a more collaborative writing process. In either case however, the complete "First Working Draft" was finished by August 12 (Scott 12).

But Campbell notes that, even then, the seeds of the eventual rift were present in the authors' difficulty with the character of Bigger Thomas. Bigger is a challenging character who kills twice, once in panic and again in cold blood. As Wright describes it in "How Bigger Was Born," the character was designed to be an experiment in what happens when you put a life into the test tubes of poverty and oppression. The result was a character type Wright had encountered throughout his life: the violent and inarticulate Bigger. To Wright, the "Biggers" of the world were the inevitable outcome of those test-tube processes.

This inevitability presented a difficulty for Green. Green believed in the Aristotelian vision of individual agency, free will, and the ultimate potential for heroism even in tragic circumstances. This capacity for agency was bound up in the character having some final say in who he is as a person. As Green wrote decades later to Houseman, he felt it was necessary that

"Bigger Thomas should come to the realization that he was at least partly responsible for the character he was and therefore had some responsibility for the fate that fell upon him" (Avery 677). This self-knowledge was what would raise Bigger to the stature of a tragic figure, not just a pathetic one, and allow the audience to learn and understand by watching "Bigger Thomas grow through his stretch of endurance and not just suffer" (Avery 677).

This difference between Bigger as a reactive product of society versus as an active agent influenced by society may not seem so vast to us, but it was apparently important enough to Green that he stipulated in his initial agreement that he be able to make such a change. We do not have a copy of this contract, but Green refers to it both in the 1973 letter to Houseman and in the interview with Wynn (Wynn, IV-10), so it is clear that, to Green at least, the possibility of growth and agency was essential to the character.

———————

By the time the "First Working Draft" was completed in August, this conflict between the scriptwriters was already most clear in the final scene of the play. As Scott notes in his chronology, while the play went through various changes in the tone, ordering, and content of the scenes between that draft and the version produced on Broadway in March 1941, none of those changes deal directly with Bigger's sense of choice and independence. Throughout most of the play, as in the novel, Bigger acts as he has been forced to act by society, often seeming as much a witness to the events as their instigator. He kills the drunken daughter of his wealthy, white employer, accidentally smothering her while trying to keep her quiet after she has lured him to her room. Later, he kills his girlfriend, fearing she will hinder his escape from the police.

For Wright, these acts of violence were the inevitable products of Bigger's upbringing and place in society. Green agreed that those forces were all-important in shaping Bigger's actions, but he believed that in the end Bigger must come to some understanding of his own responsibility. The final scene of the play was this last opportunity for Bigger to claim some sense of himself.

Given the crucial nature of this last scene, Green and Wright tried different resolutions, over several drafts of the script. In all versions of the manuscript, the play ends in Bigger's jail cell, as he confers with his lawyer. The rhetorical centerpiece of the play is the previous scene, the trial. There, Bigger is condemned to death despite the defense's argument that it is society itself that is most guilty. This leaves the final prison scene to focus on character: Bigger's own self-awareness or lack thereof. The initial draft from August ended with this self-awareness leading to a mental breakdown and Bigger crying out, "Now it come clear! I see it. All the peoples and all the killings and the hangings and the burnings, inside me, kept pushing me on — up and on to do something big — something great — to keep my head up and all the bad I done — it was right" (Green and Wright, MS1, II.vi.7).

But that scene seems to have been a placeholder even then. Notes in the first working draft include, "Ending to be changed . . . Possibility of Mrs. Dalton appearing in final scene, perhaps through her husband's power having secured a reprieve. A question of Bigger's possible suicide" (Green and Wright, MS1, II.vi.7). It is this "possible suicide" that Green first tried as a compromise between Wright's vision and his own. Bigger's suicide would, for Green, be a definitive, internally motivated choice, something that Bigger could claim for his own. And, for Wright, it would be consistent with a drive toward self-destruction indicated in the book. He wrote to Green in October, "The more I've thought of your idea of ending the play with Bigger killing himself, I like it. If you'd like my working with you to complete the ms., just say so" (Wright, Letter, Oct. 3).

That was the ending Green used as he revised the script through the fall and into the winter, moving scenes around, combining and recombining characters, and making other revisions suggested by Houseman. It was slow going, and Houseman wrote pointedly in December, seeming to threaten to delay the start of rehearsals until the script was in final. In mid-January, all four met in Philadelphia, and Green provided what he considered the final draft of the script. Confirming this, he wired Houseman on the 18th saying, "Script you received in Philadelphia may for our present purposes be

In the summer of 1940, Richard Wright and Paul Green stirred up a local controversy by working side by side on the then-segregated University of North Carolina campus. Green helped adapt Wright's novel *Native Son* for the Broadway stage. Photo by Alexander M. Rivera, courtesy of the Paul Green Foundation.

considered final but will get another marked edited copy to you at earliest convenience" (Avery 321).

In this draft, as Bigger leaves his cell, heading for the death chamber, he grabs a gun from the guard, saying, "Yeh. The last minute I saw it—the chance to do something big, something right. For you, Mr. Max, I prove myself. See, I don't kill anybody. I could shoot you all down, but I don't. I don't hate you. Another man I got to kill. Goodbye, Mr. Max." This is followed by a stage direction: "(He shoots himself through the breast. He staggers and then falls slowly down on the cot)" (Green and Wright, MS2, III.iii.11).

This second version of the ending gave Green the heroic action he felt was necessary to put Bigger's character in perspective: one single act of agency at the bitter end of his life. It is unclear what Wright himself thought of it, but Houseman was unsatisfied. Seeking a shorter running time and a different take on the ending, Houseman sat down with Wright to start trimming the script, even as rehearsals were starting. In my own career, I recognize this as the usual process between playwright and producer as a script approaches production, but the particular changes they made to the ending were significant. On February 12, Wright wrote to Green, "Houseman and I finished cutting the play. I don't know just how you will like the last scene, but we recast it in terms of the book. It is short, effective, I think, and forms a good conclusion to the play" (Wright, Letter, Feb. 12).

The ending in this draft more closely reflected Wright's own view of Bigger's character. Now, after an abbreviated discussion in the cell between Bigger and his lawyer, Mr. Max, the play ends with an extended stage direction: "(Bigger grasps the prison bars. He looks straight out holding on to the bars. Max turns away from him and walks down the corridor and off right. The lights start to fade. Bigger just stands holding on to the bars, looking straight out. The lights fade out completely. The curtain falls)" (Mantle 63).

This third ending seems strangely inert on the page, but on the stage, it is a powerful visual symbol: Bigger with his arms stretched out like Christ, staring at the society that condemned him. Maybe this is why, years later, Green seemed to feel the idea came from the director, Orson Welles. He told Wynn, "Welles walked up and down, and he said, 'No, no.' . . . So, they ended it the way they had planned, with Bigger Thomas behind the bars with his hands upheld like the crucified Jesus, I mean stretched out as if he was on the cross. And the whole thing saying at the end, 'Look, white folks, what you've done to me!' " (Wynn, IV-17-18).

But Green still felt that a compromise between these visions was possible. In the last week of February, he met with Wright in a hotel room in New York to try to hammer out a new ending. While this draft made other cuts to keep the running time Welles wanted, it restored some passages in the prison scene dealing with Bigger's developing sense of responsibility and, importantly, introduced a fourth variation on the ending. In this draft,

Bigger again takes the gun from the inattentive guard but without the intention to kill himself. He cries out, "Yeh, at the last I do it—I see my way. Now I hold your life in my hands! But I ain't going to kill you. I ain't. I give it back to you. Mr. Max! Mr. Max! Tell 'em—tell 'em—for Bigger. I died—free—at last the last—my own man," and lets the gun fall from his hand, before walking into the death house, "as if into a deep current of water" (Green and Wright, MS3, x.12).

But something happened during that last attempt at collaboration. The scene was completed on March 1, with rehearsals well under way for an opening on the 17th. According to Scott, Wright signed off on the ending, and Green returned home. But the scene never made it to the rehearsal room. Two days later, on March 3, Green sent the following telegram to his agent, Paul Reynolds:

> Since I am unable to be in New York at this time, and in order to help Native Son towards as complete a presentation as possible, I wish Wright to take over the authority as author for the production of the final scene there, and likewise I will take the authority for the published script of the last scene, the rest of the play standing in joint responsibility as is. It is understood that he and I will continue our mutual aid on the show in any and every way possible. (Avery 324)

While it is couched in Green's typically genteel language, the telegram suggests something unheard of: that the performed and published versions of a play should be deliberately different, with different authors for each.

Two weeks later, *Native Son* opened with the "crucifixion" ending. Adding another layer to the confusion, the published version of the play featured neither that ending nor the "gun renunciation," but rather a fifth version. Green did not actually attend opening night, telling Wynn that he "thought it was Richard Wright's evening" (Wynn IV-18). But when he saw the performance later in the week, it changed his perspective on the last scene. As he wrote to his agent, "After considering the method—a kind of fierce, close-up intensity—which Welles is using in producing the show, I came to the conclusion that the script had best adhere somewhat to that, since the matter of a well-rounded, well-constructed play was already through the window. So I limped the ending across the goal line as best I could" (Avery 326).

To that end, the published version of the play keeps from the "gun renunciation" the final image of Bigger walking toward the death house and the priest intoning, "I am the resurrection and the life" (148), but the defining action, the taking and dropping of the gun, is replaced by a more subtle moment. Harkening back to an earlier conversation about Bigger's dreams of being a pilot, the ending now reads as follows:

> BIGGER: (*in a fierce convulsive whisper*) There she comes—Yeh, I hear you. (*Far above in the night the murmuring throb of an airplane motor is audible. Bigger's voice bursts from him in a wild frenzied call.*) Fly them planes, boys—fly 'em!—Riding through—riding through. I'll be with you! I'll—
>
> FIRST GUARD: Come on, he's going nuts! (*He quickly unlocks the cell and they enter.*)
>
> BIGGER: (*Yelling, his head wagging in desperation*) Keep on driving!— To the end of the world—smack into the face of the sun! (Gasping) Fly 'em for me—for Bigger. (144)

Welles, apparently furious about the change, demanded that his name be removed from the dust jacket (Rowley 240). Nor does it seem to have been satisfying to Green, who would revise the ending twice more: for the play's 1965 revival (which used the gun renunciation) and for the play's North Carolina premiere in 1970. It was, in fact, the play that Green chose from all his works to open the theater named for him on the campus of the University of North Carolina at Chapel Hill. This time, a sixth version of the ending was written with input from Ellen Wright, Richard Wright's widow. Again, the play ends with Bigger striding into the death house, but instead of the gun or the planes, now there is a question and answer with Mr. Max that reflects, as Ellen Wright put it, "the dawning of his concern for himself as inextricably linked up with the fate of others, who, victims of the same inequalities, might wind up like him" (E. Wright). The heroic action is no longer an inward-facing realization or choice, but, instead, an outward connection to something larger.

For all its drama and its sudden end, the story of the collaboration is well documented by Bauer and Scott. What eluded and intrigued me was the turning point, when Green chose to publish one version and send another to Broadway. We know it haunted him and was likely at the root of his continual revisions of the ending. Bauer points out that in many interviews in his later years, Green expresses frustration (although often mixed with admiration) toward Welles and Houseman, and for the ending itself, but also regret over the way he worked with Wright. She notes that Green returned again and again in his interviews to the fact that Wright always called him "Mr. Green," and he never thought to break that hierarchy and ask him to "Call me Paul." The ending seems to have stayed with him, not just for what he felt was a failure of ideas, but the failure of a friendship.

But what of Wright? Was he manipulated by Welles and Houseman, as Green seemed to feel, or did the "crucifixion" ending better represent what he had expressed in the novel? And what of his relationship with Green? Did he also feel and mourn the end of that friendship? While Green's voluminous letters and interviews give us some insight, Wright was more silent on the matter.

But not entirely silent. The key for me turned out to be a document that Green knew of but never saw himself. In the Wynn interview, he recalls a phone call from Brooks Atkinson, the theater critic for the *New York Times* the week of *Native Son*'s opening. Atkinson expressed concern over a piece Wright wrote for the *Times* about the process of the adaptation (Wynn IV-19). Although Green doesn't mention it in that interview, Scott points out that Wright actually wired to tell Green about the piece himself (Scott 25). Green's reply was telling:

> I am sure your article for the Times is a good one, but wonder whether it is wise to make public at this time any past difference of opinion between the authors. Since the published ending is so nearly in line with the stage version except for a little cutting here and there don't you think we had better stand or fall together on the production? Later

when the play is safely established for a run or not then it won't matter so much." (Rowley 244)

Whether because of Green's urging or otherwise, the article was never published, and Green never read it (Wynn IV-19). But the piece, "The Problem of the Hero," is available in Wright's papers at the Beinecke Rare Book and Manuscript Library at Yale University. They graciously provided me with a copy when I was working on *Native*, and it served for me as the necessary lens for understanding that crucial final page of the play and the relationship between these two men.

Importantly, "The Problem of the Hero" is not the repudiation that Green feared, and possibly ruminated on in later years. It is structured as a script, in four acts, between the Black Man and the White Man, its intention spelled out in the opening stage direction: "(The following is not a verbatim report of conversations that took place between Paul Green and me, but an attempt to reconstruct the central problem we faced in dramatizing my novel, *Native Son*.)" (Wright, "Problem," 1).

The four acts follow the timeline of the adaptation from Chapel Hill, to New York, to the hotel room. In every scene the two men argue for their positions, in the dense, powerful language that Wright used in his novels, but always with grace and the faith that both are working toward the same goal. Each character concedes that the other's perspective—Green's need for a hero, Wright's need for truth—is vital to their success. And every scene ends with the hopeful belief that, given their dedication to that shared goal, they will find a solution. The final scene ends as history did, with the realization that, no matter their shared genius, they could not square that circle. But it is not for a lack of genuine feeling between the two. The final page of dialogue is particularly telling and is quoted in its entirety here:

WHITE MAN: Well, it is difficult to end this play in the manner in which you have done when we are both working so hard after the same thing.

BLACK MAN: But really, you and I, who write, who create, what will we have to say about this war, about the disposition, the distribution of wealth, about the terms of peace? Nothing. We draw our

symbols and images of art and charge into them all the feeling in
us and yet the tide of history rolls on, on steel wheels.

WHITE MAN: But we see the same vision, we want the same thing.

BLACK MAN: But there are so many men of power and money who
are different, who believe otherwise, who see otherwise. And they
stand between us. Yes, America needs men, men who control
their own destinies. You and I, black and white, wanting the same
humane values to live by, do not control our destinies — You and
I, black and white, are not yet free. So not [*sic*] matter how painful
or dissatisfying, Bigger must die the same agonizing death in the
play that he died in the novel, the same death that millions are
dying at this moment every hour of the day all over the world . . .

WHITE MAN: (sighing) Well, let us hope.

BLACK MAN: (soberly) Yes, we must hope, for it is all we have.

WHITE MAN: But there must be heroes!

BLACK MAN: There shall be heroes, when men are free!

*(They shake hands and depart, each to think and feel and work for the day
when heroes of the people shall be born to America.)* (Wright, "The Problem of the Hero," 7)

Wright had written an ending, not for Bigger, but for the two of them.
In it, there is shared respect and eloquent argument. But Green never saw
it. Instead, the last time they were in the same room was in that hotel, and
instead of the handshake, they ended with the two different versions of the
script. Reading that, I realized my play wasn't about adapting a novel, or
even about race and privilege. It was about the end of a friendship. As my
version of Green tells Wright, "Dick, you're young, so maybe you haven't
realized this before. But allow me this one piece of advice to you. Not every
friendship can survive the artistic process."

Ultimately, the Broadway production of *Native Son* was a success, but not
the one any of its creators expected. Welles told the cast he thought it would
run at least three years. Instead, it ran ninety-seven performances, followed
by a national tour—a solid showing, but nothing approaching the blockbuster the novel had been. Critical response to the play praised Welles's

swift direction and Canada Lee's portrayal of Bigger but was generally negative about the writing. Critics found fault with Bigger's "uncharacteristic eloquence" and an ending that "scarcely explains" the changes in Bigger (Lockridge; Kronenberg). It is unclear though if any of the other versions of the ending would have addressed or worsened these critiques.

For the writers though, it was a topic they could never quite leave behind. Presumably still seeking a successful adaptation, Wright went on to make a film of *Native Son*, writing the screenplay with producer Pierre Chenal. When Canada Lee was unable to play Bigger, Wright took on that role as well. But the film was less successful than the play, ending in a financial loss for Wright (Scott 29).

And, as mentioned previously, Green would return to the end of the play in two other versions, and to the end of the friendship in numerous interviews. As Bauer points out, the privilege and authority he had in the development process was something he didn't seem to fully realize until years later. And when he did, he seems to have regretted his actions, and what he felt was lost. A lifelong champion of Black rights and communities, he was still a product of the South in the mid-twentieth century.

I wonder though if he would have felt differently had he read "The Problem of the Hero." Would he have been relieved to read Wright's version of the story of these two men, conflicted but full of respect? How might that regret have lifted had he seen those two men, one Black, one white, shake hands and depart, each to think and feel and work for the day when heroes of the people shall be born to America?

I was tempted to bring that into the play but wanted to confine myself to the events of that March night, when we know they did not resolve the question. It would have been wrong to grant them a "happy ending" so outside the facts we know. On the other hand, in the film based on the play, *The Problem of the Hero*, which EBZB Productions released in 2023, the script was opened up and actually included part of Wright's "Problem." On-screen, in scenes with other characters, there was room to explore the respect these men had for each other and their shared desire to bridge the divide.

But the film ends as history did, with Richard Wright surrounded by the jewels and furs of a Broadway opening and Green alone in his home in Chapel Hill, preparing the publisher's manuscript. Each had won an artistic victory but perhaps had lost something more valuable.

"That Better Way to Find"

Adapting Paul Green's Antiwar Play, *Johnny Johnson*

When the Paul Green Foundation asked me in early 2021 to adapt Green's 1936 antiwar play *Johnny Johnson* for a modern audience, I was both honored and daunted. How to make changes to the work of such a renowned playwright? Where to start? The story of how the play was created and Green's collaboration with composer Kurt Weill and the historic Group Theatre of New York is fascinating. Figuring out how to respect the work of these legendary artists while still making the play more producible and relevant for today's audience was a humbling and exciting undertaking.

Although the play, originally produced by the Group Theatre, was runner-up for a New York Drama Critics' Award in 1937 and had been produced many times since then in the United States and Europe, it had been out of print for decades. Samuel French published the original script, *Johnny Johnson (The Biography of a Common Man)*, in 1936 and Green's revised script in 1971. The Paul Green Foundation, which holds copyright for all of Green's published works, had a version of the play as a Word document. However, it appeared to be a mishmash of more than one version. (Paul Green was known to fiddle with all his plays, even after publication and productions.)

The Green Foundation found that producers' interest in the play rose during the years spanning the one hundredth anniversary of World War I. Because the play is long (the 1936 script runs 175 pages; the 1971 version runs 122 pages) and has many set changes and a large cast, some companies requested cuts. Such changes require negotiating and led to the Foundation's desire to publish its own shorter adaptation. Foundation board members also believed that judicious cuts would help move the story along and emphasize the character of Johnny Johnson, a young soldier trying to do what was right under horrific circumstances.

Johnny was drawn from Green's own experiences during World War I. Like many Americans at the time, Green was against the United States joining the war; he believed, as President Woodrow Wilson did, that neutrality was the correct path. However, after Germany's sinking of several ships and announcing it would renew unrestricted submarine warfare, President Wilson publicly spoke in favor of the U.S. joining the war effort. In his address to Congress on April 2, 1917, Wilson said, "It is a fearful thing to lead this great peaceful people . . . into the most terrible and disastrous of all wars. . . . But more precious than peace . . . we shall fight for the things which we have always carried nearest our hearts—for democracy." Wilson said this would be the war "to end all wars."

These words resonated deeply with Green, and he enlisted in the U.S. Army that very month, serving with the 105th Engineers, 30th Division. Green has the character of Johnny read part of Wilson's speech: "We have no quarrel with the German people" (Green, *Johnny* 32). Wilson's next line, "We have no feeling towards them but one of sympathy and friendship" is illustrated when Johnny spares the life of a young German soldier, a pivotal moment in the play that will determine the fate of both.

It cannot be overstated how devastating World War I was. From 1914 to 1919, the number of military and civilian casualties was around twenty million deaths and twenty-one million wounded. About two-thirds of military deaths were in battle and about one-third from disease, including the 1918 flu pandemic and deaths while held as prisoners of war. Green's letters to family members and the diary he kept from the spring of 1917 until June 1919 include detailed descriptions of training-camp life, combat in France and Belgium, and his time in Paris shortly after the war. He was discouraged by the infighting among the troops, the tedium and endless cigarette smoking between shell bursts, the existential threat of poison gas attacks, and the seeming ineptitude and callousness of the generals who saw the soldiers as so much fodder. All of these moments are portrayed in *Johnny Johnson*.

After the war, Green returned to the University of North Carolina at Chapel Hill, where he began his playwriting career under the tutelage of

Brother Hugh Green (left) and Paul Green managed to see each other briefly in 1918 during their service in World War I. Their harrowing experiences in the trenches of France and Belgium inspired Paul to write the antiwar musical *Johnny Johnson*, commissioned by the Group Theatre and produced in 1936 with music by Kurt Weill and some lyrics by Elizabeth Green. Photo courtesy of the Paul Green Foundation.

Professor Fred Koch, the founder of Carolina Playmakers. Green went on to become a professor there, and he continued to write plays and screenplays as well as essays, short stories, novels, and letters throughout his lifetime. It was decades after World War I before he drew on his wartime experiences to write *Johnny Johnson*.

Johnny Johnson spans two decades, from 1917 to 1936, following the life of a cheerful, naive, yet thoughtful Everyman. (Green chose the name Johnny Johnson because it was the most common name of American soldiers in the war.) The play opens with Johnny, a tombstone carver, presenting his monument to peace in the village square. He is looking forward to a life with his beloved Minny Belle. Just as the monument is to be unveiled, the mayor reports that war has been declared and all able-bodied men should enlist. Johnny initially refuses to join up, despite pressure from Minny Belle, but after reading President Wilson's speech asking Congress to support sending troops to Europe, Johnny decides to enlist. Minny Belle is thrilled. Although she sings a love song to Johnny, later we see that perhaps she is more in love with the idea of herself as the pining sweetheart of a war hero.

Johnny is sent to the front lines, where he volunteers for missions but never shoots his gun. Despite witnessing the daily horrors, fear, tedium, and slaughter of war, he never stops believing that ordinary, good people can make a difference, and he tries to stop further bloodshed. Those he encounters along the way believe he is simpleminded, even insane, while the audience sees he is wrestling with profound questions: What is democracy? Why do we fight and kill rather than communicate and debate? Johnny meets a young German soldier and convinces him to send a letter to his commander asking that the soldiers stop fighting. Later, after Johnny is wounded in battle, he sneaks into a meeting of the Allied generals to convince them to sign an order to stop an impending battle. The terrible battle ensues, however, and shortly thereafter Johnny is arrested. Suffering from "shell shock" (what we now know as PTSD), he is sent to a "House of Balm," an asylum for wounded veterans.

Johnny lives in the asylum for ten years and uses his carving skills to make wooden toys. The inmates, led by Johnny, establish their own version of a League of Nations, with the goal of creating a society that values peaceful resolution to conflicts. When Johnny finally is released, he discovers that Minny Belle has married his rival, Anguish Howington, now a wealthy businessman. His village in Act One has grown into a city, and the Great Depression has left its mark. Johnny tries to make a living by selling his wooden toys on the street. A parade is beginning, and in the background, we hear bombastic talk of war, patriotism, and "America First," the rumblings of what would become the next world war. The play ends with Johnny singing a sad and hopeful song as he calls out into the dark streets, "Toys! Toy-ees for sale!"

Green collaborated on *Johnny Johnson* with the Group Theatre, a socially progressive theater collective based in New York and formed in 1931 by

Harold Clurman, Cheryl Crawford, and Lee Strasberg. They wanted to produce work that was original, naturalistic, and edgy. They had produced Green's play *The House of Connelly* in 1931 and wanted to work with him again. When German composer Kurt Weill, who had written *The Three-penny Opera*, moved to New York with his wife Lotte Lenya, fleeing Nazi Germany, the Group was eager to collaborate with Green. Crawford introduced Weill to Green, since she knew both wrote about common people defying the powerful elite, which aligned with the Group's mission as well. The three of them came up with the idea of a play about an ordinary soldier in World War I. Green said he'd had the idea of a play about "an ordinary simple soldier who hated war" (Crawford 94). Green said he'd had the idea of writing a play based on his war experiences for some time.

Crawford, Green, and Weill discussed George Büchner's play *Woyzeck*, Jaroslav Hašek's novel *The Good Soldier Švejk*, and Carl Zuckmayer's play *The Captain of Köpenick*. These works featured soldiers caught up in the cruelty of war. Green had traveled in Europe and liked the theater he saw there, which was edgier than the offerings in the United States. He wanted to use spectacle and music to tell a humanistic story about a common man. Crawford rented a house in the country near New York for them to work together. Ethan Mordden wrote that although the Group and Green thought musicals were dramatically unworthy, "this one was not only politically interesting but artistically innovative" (185).

The collaboration was thorny, to put it mildly. Timothy Carter wrote in a program note for the Chicago Folks Operetta's 2017 production of *Johnny Johnson*: "Green found the writing difficult: although he was in general interested in the uses of music in the theater, he struggled with how songs might work within dramatic action. Weill, too, had problems adjusting to the conventions of American musical theater" (Review). Green wrote that although they had fun working together, "Usually [Weill] was fanning down my neck with his score for he was wonderfully prolific, and I'd try to stay ahead of him. Sometimes, though, he would get ahead and would write a melody which he liked, and I would then have the devil of a time trying to create a lyric to fit it" (Green, *Plough*, 54). Mordden claimed that "Green . . . kept hogging the center of the writing, leaving the score at the edges of the narration" (184). In an email to me, Paul Green scholar Laurence

Avery expressed his belief that Green and Weill were "writing songs for their friends." As Mordden writes, "If too much of the score gives solos to minor characters, that does support Green's kaleidoscopic approach: except for Johnny, the show consists of an ever-changing *dramatis personae*. Highlighting these starry bit parts, Weill gave them pastiche numbers" (185). The script "progressed slowly" according to Crawford, who referred to its "daily agonies" (94–95). To complicate matters further, Green and Lenya (Weill's wife) purportedly became romantically involved.

Crawford agonized over the numerous production and financial problems. "The show . . . had nineteen sets, some of them enormous. Dress rehearsals were a shambles and much more expensive than I had counted on. . . . The sets . . . overpowered the actors," none of whom were trained singers. During previews, "We communicated . . . mostly by screams, our faces withered with strain" (Crawford 96). In the end, the Group billed *Johnny Johnson* as "A Play with Music," perhaps admitting, Mordden writes, that "it wasn't anything like a musical" (185). The show opened at New York's Weber and Fields Music Hall in November 1936 and closed after sixty-eight performances. It received some good reviews, especially, according to Carter, by leftist reviewers, who gave it some credit for its "theatrical daring."

To prepare for revising the script, I kept Cheryl Crawford's observations in mind and read whatever I could find about productions of the play. I read both published versions several times, including Green's own annotated copy of the 1971 version, and consulted the Kurt Weill critical edition edited by Timothy Carter (2012), which includes the entire text and score. I read Green's war diaries and poems as well as war poems by Wilfred Owen and Isaac Rosenberg. I also watched films about World War I such as *A Farewell to Arms*, *All Quiet on the Western Front*, *Paths of Glory*, and *1917*, as well as *Woyzeck*, based on Georg Büchner's "dramatic fragment" that Green, Weill, and Crawford had discussed when shaping *Johnny Johnson*. I listened repeatedly to Weill's score, both the MGM record with Burgess Meredith as Johnny (orchestra conducted by Samuel Matlowsky), and a later recording on CD by the Otaré Pit Band (conducted by Joel Cohen). I also looked at playbills and promotional pieces from various productions of the play.

I had several goals: First, to shorten the running time by cutting nonessential dialogue, characters, or scenes. Second, to suggest ways that fewer actors could portray the more than forty characters by double or triple casting. Third, to keep most of Weill's music if it carried the story forward or created or sustained a mood. Fourth, to keep the flavor of Green's dialogue, including its humor and (often dated) slang, to help bring out the character of Johnny as naive but not stupid. Fifth, to keep the style that Green intended: Act One as comedy, Act Two as tragedy, Act Three as satire. Ultimately, I did shape the play into two acts rather than three, as the three acts were uneven in length and one intermission seemed sufficient.

I tried always to be mindful of Green's and Weill's intentions. Similar to Johnny's work as a stone carver, my work would primarily be to chisel away parts that made the story lag or go off in directions that did not serve the play overall. As I will discuss later, I did add a few touches that I felt were in keeping with the spirit of the play.

With more than thirty songs and multiple sets, the original runs more than three hours. Though the dialogue is at turns funny, thoughtful, and occasionally sublime, other parts are corny and dated or go on longer than necessary. Except for Johnny, most of the characters are superficial and unsympathetic—this is primarily a satirical work. Some of these characters I minimized or deleted. Also, the elaborate stage directions, though at times poetic, are overly instructive (e.g., stating the exact placement of each character onstage or how an actor should portray an emotion), so those were shortened.

Clearing out scenes or characters that did not advance the narrative helped Johnny's character come through more strongly. At times the dialogue undercut his childlike wisdom and made him appear as a simpleminded rube, in the vein of the 1960s television sitcom *Gomer Pyle, U.S.M.C.* This was especially true in a scene of him undergoing basic training; I cut that scene entirely. Charlie Chaplin's Tramp was a better model for Johnny, and Green did write, "No doubt Johnny owes a lot to Chaplin" (Avery 689). Green also said that he considered Johnny to be like the folksy storyteller Will Rogers, with whom he'd worked in Hollywood (Avery 684).

Deciding which songs could be eliminated was tough. I listened to Weill's score every day for weeks and fell in love with most of the songs, even those that seemed irrelevant to the story. There were eighteen songs in Act I, thirteen in Act II (some of which are musical interludes). Keeping in mind the pacing, mood, and relevance of the songs helped in deciding which songs were necessary. For example, Act I, Scene 1 has three songs in the first six pages—before we even learn that war has been declared, which kicks off the plot. I kept these songs because they launch the rest of the story, though suggesting they could be shortened; a contemporary audience would quickly grow restless. In Scene 2 "The Treadle Song" is sung by a minor character and has nothing to do with the rest of the story. Scene 3 has a wonderful tango sung by a sleazy Captain Valentine, also a minor character, which also is distracting to the story. In Act II, Scene 2, "The Cowboy Song," sung by one of the American soldiers at the Front, felt unnecessary. These songs were jettisoned.

The other two songs in that scene stayed in. "The Tea Song" adds a lighter note and brief respite in the otherwise grim war scene. The eerie "Song of the Guns" follows. This song sets up the next pivotal scene, when Johnny encounters a young German soldier whose life he spares. Powerful, innovative, and haunting pieces, such as the "Song of the Goddess," "Song of the Guns," and "Song of the Wounded Frenchmen," are essential to the mood and story and are deeply effective, as are the musical interludes between scenes.

Another problematic part of the play is in the scene at the asylum, where Johnny finds not only peace but camaraderie and purpose among his fellow inmates. These wounded veterans live in a world of their own, alternating between drowsiness and creating their own version of the League of Nations. The idea makes a good satire, but most of their dialogue depends on the audience knowing who the characters represent in the real League of Nations. Green uses quotes and stage directions that describe the actual representatives. None of this is recognizable to a modern audience. In the adaptation, this dialogue has been pared down to the essential idea: that these supposedly insane men continue to work for peace and harmony as brothers.

This adaptation suggests double (and occasionally triple) casting so the number of actors can be minimized from forty to about twelve. In keeping with the idea of spectacle, Green had included many characters with no or few speaking parts, as villagers, soldiers, members of the Allied High

Command, guards, and inmates. With modern technology, these characters can be suggested by using projected films or stills from the era and innovative lighting (for the battle scenes, for example) to create the illusion of more characters onstage.

Flexible casting also would allow for more diverse characters. The play takes place when citizens of Johnny's southern hometown and troops would have been segregated. The most diversity is in scenes with the soldiers who represent white immigrant Americans, English soldiers, the Europeans in the Allied High Command, and occasionally a German enemy. Of course, nontraditional casting—choosing the best actor for a given role without considering race, gender, or ethnicity—is now popular. The play has only four speaking roles for women, none of which have much substance. However, roles written for men can be played by women, such as doctors, attendants, stenographers, soldiers. A diverse cast can remind us that the issues of authoritarianism, divisiveness, and the trauma of war reach beyond the scope of World War I and, indeed, are with us today.

In the final scene in the new adaptation, I wanted to make more explicit some consequences that Green had hinted at. When Johnny is released from the asylum, we now see that the bustling town where he tries to sell his toys was once his village from Act I, scene 1. It is 1936, during the Great Depression, and a jingoistic parade is underway. A loudmouthed orator urges "America First" to a drumbeat. We are witnessing the rise of fascism and another war in the making. Johnny, alone and a stranger in his own town, encounters Minny Belle, who has married Johnny's rival, Anguish Howington. She is wealthy and complacent, with a child in tow. The boy wants to buy a toy soldier, but Johnny doesn't make them. The boy gives Johnny a nickel anyway. (In the adaptation, a sad man in ragged clothes enters, and Johnny gives him the nickel.) Johnny's bleak return to his hometown, where he once dreamed of a loving and peaceful life, illustrates Thomas Wolfe's remark, "You can't go home again." To emphasize that this was once his village, I have Johnny uncover a monument that has been draped with an "America First" banner. He gently polishes the stone, and we see the word *Peace*; it is his monument from the first scene. The play ends with Johnny trying to sell his toys on the empty streets and singing "Johnny's Song."

Carter noted that Johnny's last song has "a beguiling sincerity that is all the more powerful for its time, with another world war on the horizon. It is a quite remarkable work" (Review). Green, however, had mixed feelings about "Johnny's Song." In a 1975 letter to Crawford, he wrote that he "struggled . . . to find a bigger and better statement of man's dilemma of war and peace to conclude with. But I failed. . . . The words of this song are not too good." He added that in his 1971 revision, "I improved Johnny's final peace song. . . . I have him sing it dynamically and in opposition to the distant harangue of the military demagogue . . . the harangue gradually weakening as Johnny sings out his message of good will" (Avery 681–82). My hopes for this adapted script are that Johnny's character shines through, the story is told clearly in Green's voice, and Weill's music is used effectively and movingly. In *Johnny Johnson*, we see how well-meaning, ordinary citizens who are manipulated to kill in the name of patriotism must live with the aftermath. Johnny does not give up his ideals or become jaded despite the darkness of the times.

Green was well aware that his antiwar theme would resonate beyond the time frame of World War I. He subtitled *Johnny Johnson* "The Biography of a Common Man" and dedicated it to "A Memory Living." He established the time for the play as "A few years ago as well as now."

As Carter wrote, the playwright "published a cut-down version of the text; he then revised it for staging in 1956 (after Weill's death) and in 1971. But he was never entirely happy with the result" (Carter, Program notes). It is noteworthy that these revisions coincided with the Cold War and later the Vietnam War, when the public was anxious about the United States' involvement and the news reported body counts daily. The play being set "a few years ago as well as now" resonated as I researched and worked on this adaptation. At the time *Johnny Johnson* opened in November 1936, Franklin D. Roosevelt was reelected by the greatest plurality in American history, and the New Deal was underway. When OdysseyStage in Chapel Hill, North Carolina, did a staged reading of the adapted script in May 2022, former president Donald Trump, an "America First" promoter, was still falsely and loudly claiming that he won the election. The January 6 insurrection showed us the fragility of our democracy. We were (and are) still feeling the effects of Covid on our society. Disinformation proliferates on the internet. Bills are passed that deny freedoms we once considered in-alienable. When Johnny's monument to peace was draped in the "America First" banner, the Chapel Hill audience was reminded of the many statues of segregationists being pulled down after long years of protests. Russia's invasion of Ukraine was (and of this writing, still is) horrifying the world every day. Green's ideas, as manifested in *Johnny Johnson*, ask us not to turn away from reality yet also not to give up hope, to keep fighting for the values of honesty and decency:

> We know there's something still
> Of good beyond such ill
> Within our heart and mind.
> We'll never lose our faith and hope
> And trust in all mankind,
> We'll work and strive
> While we're alive
> That better way to find.

Paul Green and James Boyd

The Best of Friends during the Jim Crow Era

Paul Green was a longtime friend of writer James Boyd and his family in Southern Pines, North Carolina. Boyd (1888–1944) met Green sometime after Green's star was rising as the writer of such plays as *The No 'Count Boy* (1925) and the Pulitzer winner *In Abraham's Bosom* (1927). Green's first mention of Boyd comes in a 1932 letter to writer Laurence Stallings where he describes Boyd's notoriously bad handwriting, how it was composed of wavy lines rolling across the sheet with an occasional dash, dot, or loop: "Jim has ruined my eyes with his letter. He is such an artist that he makes me want to read what he says, and he's such a master of the foxhounds that he makes the trail to find it out eye-blinding" (Avery 204).

On the surface, Green and Boyd seemed completely different, yet they grew to love one another, both of them gifted with dynamic personalities that attracted people to them. Green wrote of Boyd, "We could talk about all the things that filled our minds—books, and the joy and delight of creating them—all the craftsmen's talk we understood from each other so well" (qtd. in "Memory" 17). More than any other writer, he shared with Boyd a love of the same cultural landscape, a place that for all its challenges still inspired and informed their work.

Boyd had a complicated sense of identity and entitlement. He was from the North but identified as a southerner, lived in a plantation-style mansion, and spoke at times with a southern drawl. Green was a North Carolina native who had a clearer understanding of who he was as a person. He had great empathy for others and sought to move beyond the limitations of his rural upbringing. Boyd was more inclined to live within the constraints

of his world, while Green grabbed the lightning rod and braved the consequences. Neither of them completely left their past behind, which shaped
their actions and creative output.

An aristocrat of vast wealth, Boyd was originally from Harrisburg,
Pennsylvania, and was named for his paternal grandfather, a coal and rail-
road magnate. His family came to Southern Pines around 1904 and began
developing the resort. On the eastern edge of their property, they built the
Highland Pines Inn, its guest book reading like the society pages of the
New York Times. On five hundred acres surrounding the inn they created
Weymouth Heights, a residential subdivision with world-class amenities,
including golf and equestrian sports.

Green was also a developer. In 1933, he began creating the Greenwood
neighborhood on 212 wooded acres outside Chapel Hill. His vision was for a
community living in harmony with nature. He laid out the road himself, following the natural contours of the rolling forest and meadowland. The concept for Greenwood was likely inspired, at least in part, by the Weymouth
Heights subdivision. Created predominantly in the 1920s and '30s, the subdivision featured curving streets that corresponded to the elevations of the
ridges and wrapped around large wooded lots with native flora. Weymouth
Heights was publicized nationally through culturally persuasive magazines
such as *Country Life in America*, where Boyd had served as an editor.

His sprawling estate, called Weymouth Woods, was a gathering place
for writers in the 1920s and '30s, all of them white and most of them men.
He often invited nationally prominent authors for craft discussions and
overnight stays. Guests included Sherwood Anderson, William Faulkner,
F. Scott Fitzgerald, John Galsworthy, and Thomas Wolfe, among others.
Paul Green became a frequent guest at the estate and forged a lifelong tie
with the local community.

By 1920, Boyd and his wife, Katharine, were living full-time at Weymouth, where he began writing in earnest while also enjoying the resort
community and surrounding woodlands. His affluence marked him as different, prompting the writer Sherwood Anderson to say in a 1937 letter to
Scribner's editor Maxwell Perkins, "So here you have this man, rich, with a
big estate, a huge pack of fox-hounds, the sort of people about who go in for

After James Boyd's death, Paul Green (*left*) worked with North Carolina Poet Laureate Sam Ragan (*right*) and Boyd's widow, Katharine Lamont Boyd (1896–1974), to turn the Boyds' Southern Pines home, built in 1922, into a center for the arts and humanities. In 1979 Paul Green gave the first major gift toward the project. This photo was taken on the grounds of Weymouth Center, which is also home to the North Carolina Literary Hall of Fame. Photo courtesy of the Paul Green Foundation.

fox-hunting, all rich, decked out in their white pants and red coats . . . the whole thing seeming in some way so absurd . . . so far away from anything that matters" (Jones 371).

Known for historical fiction, Boyd's novels include *Drums* (1925) and *Marching On* (1927). Set in Edenton, North Carolina, *Drums* has been called the best novel written about the American Revolution. Its main character is Johnny Fraser, who stands helpless against the rolling tide of war, where he sees only waste, cruelty, and disruption. *Marching On* tells the story of James Fraser, a descendant of characters in *Drums*, who struggles as a Confederate soldier during the Civil War while infatuated with the daughter of a nearby plantation owner.

Boyd's interest in historical fiction was inspired by a belief that people were best understood by taking a long view of human experience and that by connecting with the past we gain insight for the present. He was particularly fascinated by southern history and native folk, whose manner of living seemed both exotic and familiar. While he was attracted by the lingering charm of the Old South, he knew that it had to change. This historical sense governed his choice of material, allowing him to comment on humanity with great depth.

Green told southern stories as well but was more pointed in his depictions of racism. From childhood, Green had seen the injustice inflicted on those less fortunate than he was. This sparked in him an abiding interest in using his craft to affect social change. From a white man's perspective, he crafted dramatic works that incorporated Black characters and attempted to show the intricacies of their lives. His one-act play, *Hymn to the Rising Sun* (1935), is a fine example of his use of art as advocacy. The drama challenged North Carolina's abusive treatment of prisoners, especially Black people, and the use of chain gangs as a form of punishment.

Green's background was so very different from Boyd's. Born in neighboring Harnett County to a family of modest means, he was raised on a farm amid poverty and the lingering effects of the Civil War. Prior to the war, his family had enslaved as many as thirty people, and their relative affluence ended at the close of war. Green said,

> Depression was just a familiar condition to me and I had been writing lots of stories and one act plays about the tenant farmers and about the Negro and all of those plays and stories or playlets sang the song of poverty, of depression, of almost disfranchisement, of lack of opportunity, of the squeeze of economic serfdom. . . . [T]here were a lot of old soldiers around and I would hear their stories, the shadow of that great foolish tragedy. . . . I understood the reasons for our condition, why there was so much poverty in eastern North Carolina. (Hall 2–4)

The Sandhills was the territory both Green and Boyd loved, a distinctive geographic region meandering through eight of the state's southeastern counties including Harnett, Green's home county, and Moore, where Boyd lived, with miles upon miles of longleaf pines set along sandy ridges that had once been the shore of an ancient sea. The soil was too poor for anything but subsistence farming, so people learned to live on the land by bleeding pines of their resin for turpentine, tar, and pitch. This left behind a wasteland as the forest was all but leveled. The Boyd family intentionally saved the oldest vestige of virgin longleaf when founding their estate, marking the point when the region turned away from the axe. Green, on the other hand, had experienced the dirty, intensive labor of turpentine, tar, and pitch extraction on his family farm.

Another bond between them was their experience of childhood illnesses. Boyd's frailty as a child made it necessary for him to be schooled at home until age twelve, and he later suffered from infantile paralysis. At age eight, Green was treated for "white swelling," an inflammation of bone tissue resulting from a fall from an apple tree. Once considered incurable, Green's joints progressively became so stiff that he could barely walk. He was finally taken to Johns Hopkins in Baltimore where they wanted to amputate his arm. His mother refused, so they operated on him without anesthesia. The surgery was a success, but the memory of excruciating pain forever haunted him.

Both writers served in the military, a recurring subject in their correspondence. As veterans of Woodrow Wilson's "war to end all wars," both men had experienced the brutality of battle. Green survived several months of heavy combat in the trenches of Belgium and France, and Boyd served in the Army Ambulance Service in Europe. Boyd's health worsened during the war, and he spent months hospitalized in recovery, resulting in lingering physical issues that would plague him for the rest of his life.

By the end of the war, racial tension was mounting. Black soldiers returned home with a deeper appreciation of their civil rights but faced state and local laws enacted to maintain white supremacy. Paul Green recounted life in the Jim Crow South in his play *In Abraham's Bosom*, where his protagonist Abraham McCranie proclaimed, "We want our children and our grandchildren to march towards full lives and noble characters" (63). And for that, he says, "We got to be free, freedom of the soul and freedom of the mind" (78).

The relationship between Green and Boyd developed during the Jim Crow era. For all its grandeur, Southern Pines was a white-dominated enclave that depended on institutionalized racism. The use of slurs to describe people of color was a common practice, even in the newspaper. For the most part, Black people stayed in West Southern Pines, a separate Black municipality established in 1923, or they lived on some of the bigger estates as servants. At the nearby Pinehurst Resort, Black and Jewish people were completely barred from living in the village.

Against this backdrop, a "writing colony" evolved in the Sandhills. Along with Boyd, Green was a well-known local figure among the writers attracted by the allure of Weymouth. Both writers topped a list of the most interesting North Carolinians in a 1929 survey conducted by the *Pilot*, a local newspaper. The two men used their celebrity status and literary voices to influence public opinion at a pivotal point in history, and as friends they navigated shifting social currents, sometimes successfully, other times not.

Their views on race and class were evolving at a time when civil rights legislation was decades away. A look at their Weymouth social circle provides insight into the racial prejudice that encompassed their lives. In particular, two writers in their literary orbit stood out for displaying the sort of ignorance that Green railed against: author Katharine Ball Ripley (1898–1955), a socialite who came to the region during the back-to-the-land movement in the 1920s; and journalist Bion H. Butler (1857–1935), editor of the *Pilot* from 1920 to 1935 and a friend of Boyd's whose estate bordered his property.

Katharine Ripley was the author of *Sand in My Shoes* (1931), a book that chronicles her experience as a Sandhills peach grower amid the extravagance of the wealthy on country estates around Pinehurst. In her narrative, Ripley characterizes Black people as ignorant and dishonest. For example, she writes about the accidental death of her sharecropper's son from a self-inflicted gunshot, an incident she also turned into a "funny story" shared at dinner parties in front of Black servants, while admitting to feeling "heartily ashamed" of herself (Ripley 279). In his review of Ripley's work, Bion Butler called the book one of "the most clever and entertaining things" produced by the writing colony" (2).

Butler was seen as a leader in the newspaper industry for nearly forty years and had served as vice president of the North Carolina Press Association. In the *Pilot*, he sometimes referred to formerly enslaved people as "old darkies," and in his 1933 book, *Old Bethesda*, he described the institution of slavery as an improvement of the condition of Black people over the "barbarism" they experienced in Africa:

> The Northerner man can see how it is possible to be considerate of his dog or his horse or his cattle, but he has deluded himself with the notion that the Southern white man was not considerate of his negro, a property much greater than that of a dog or horse, and a human creature who awakened in his white folks a sincere friendship that the Northern white people have never been able to comprehend. (187–88)

According to Butler, the idealisms of the North led to the creation of the Ku Klux Klan, noting that "actual killings" were rare in the Sandhills. He said that a contributing factor was the intellectual inferiority of Black people: "It was impossible that the South should do anything after the Civil War but retain the authority of the intelligent white man of business ability and experience over the intrusion of the submerged minority into political management" (198). Butler repeated such racist views over and over, nearly verbatim, in *The Pilot* and other newspapers.

While no evidence has surfaced showing that Green directly challenged anyone in the writing colony, he spoke out against the prejudice expressed by people like Ripley and Butler. In describing his early efforts for social change and civil rights, he said:

> We've had three hundred years of Negro talent, great voices, possible mighty singers, mighty poets, doctors, all gone to oblivion. I don't suppose that half a dozen out of the 14 million that have lived and died in North Carolina, just to give an illustration, hardly half a dozen reached their full maturity and power. Only a few, and they could have. I guess that there is nothing as sinful as a man, is there, as a human being. The greatest sin, I guess, is to cause another person to miss his life, because he has missed all. And we have caused so many people to miss their lives. (Hall 41)

James Boyd was a contributing editor for the *Pilot* in the 1930s, and he also wrote the introduction to Butler's *Old Bethesda*. In the introduction, Boyd describes a carriage ride with his grandmother to the nearby Bethesda

Presbyterian Church. He compares her strong religious beliefs to those of the Sandhills natives. He goes on to describe the sanctuary as a place where trials had been held for those who acted against church doctrine. The punishment for such crimes was banishment from the congregation, and the fear of being left without a fold controlled church members. An aversion to being excluded might account for Boyd's own willingness to follow the status quo, that and a failure to anticipate the repercussions of his actions.

Roderick Brower, great nephew of Hilton Walker, a servant at Weymouth, spent time with his uncle at the estate. "James Boyd had a kind heart," he says. Hilton Walker started as a gardener, advancing to butler and chauffeur. His relatives remember him as a gentleman of refined taste, "like all the others at Weymouth." His great-nephew spoke of Walker's admiration for his employer:

> My uncle loved Boyd and loved working for him. He had empathy for his Black servants, his quote-unquote friends, but he still turned a blind eye to them when it came to retaining his social status. It's unsettling to know he stood by people like Katharine Ripley and Bion Butler. That they would refer to someone as "old darkie" cuts deep. We weren't seen as human, just things to be used. All these years later there are still people that feel this way. My education, profession and income—none of it matters. They think I'm less than them because of my race. (Brower, personal interview)

In addition to Boyd, other members of the writing colony were contributing editors for the *Pilot* in the early to mid-1930s. This included novelist and poet Struthers Burt, his wife Katharine, a novelist and writer of screenplays, writer Ralph W. Page, and Maud Parker Child and Almet Jenks, regular contributors to the *Saturday Evening Post*.

Green was not a contributor to the *Pilot*, but he was regularly featured in the paper and in other county news outlets during the 1930s. His work was the subject of book club meetings and forums at local country clubs that featured readings from his early plays. Local schools and amateur theater groups performed his plays, such as *Fixin's*, *The Last of the Lowries*, *No 'Count Boy*, and *Quare Medicine*. The society pages gave accounts of prominent citizens attending performances of his plays across the state, including the county sheriff. In 1934, a local woman named Mary Fowler Spencer played the lead role in Green's *Shroud My Body Down* at Playmakers Theater in Chapel Hill.

While Green was a celebrated figure in his native Sandhills during the 1930s, at this point in time his work did little if anything to mitigate racial prejudice in the community. A closer look at the activities of his Sandhills associates in the 1930s sheds light on the challenge he faced in reaching hearts and minds, including instances where his friend James Boyd disregarded the rights and dignity of Black people.

In 1931, Boyd joined Bion Butler and others to advocate for the annexation of West Southern Pines by the town of Southern Pines. Black leaders were not consulted, and residents were split in their opinions, some feeling they would have endured any hardship to remain free of annexation. Boyd said his primary concern was public welfare with the onset of the Great Depression. He was actively using his own resources to provide food, clothing, and financial relief to economically challenged white and Black citizens through his service on the Planning Committee of the Unemployment Fund.

New York City's *Dunbar News* reported the annexation as a cynical attempt to control Black people, suggesting the measure was unconstitutional, with Southern Pines town records confirming that the move was instigated in part to benefit the resort, which was "dependent upon the negroes as servants" ("Southern Pines"). As a follow-up, Boyd wrote to the New York Citizens Union, saying the Black town had been a self-governing ghetto with rampant crime and inadequate public facilities, where taxes weren't honestly collected or utilized. He reported improvements to sewers, water supply, and policing after the takeover, admitting this did little to address the social, economic, and political problems in his still-segregated town.

The problems lingered, and the years following the annexation were characterized by mistrust, resentment, and misunderstanding. People from West Southern Pines provided much of the labor that built the town and worked at resorts and private homes, yet it would be more than three decades before the larger municipality added a Black police officer, integrated schools, or welcomed Black people at the bowling alley and golf courses; before they didn't have to sit in the balcony or at the back, use segregated drinking fountains and restrooms, could try on clothes in a downtown shop, and gained representation on the town council. Well into the 1950s there were unpaved streets, no sidewalks, and few if any services in West Southern Pines, even though white leaders gave the impression it was necessary to take over the area because these improvements were needed. According to Roderick Brower, "The annexation of West Southern Pines didn't significantly improve the community for more than thirty years, yet people's rights were taken away. They were stripped of their dignity and Boyd played a part in it."

In the annexation's aftermath, white town leaders endeavored to improve race relations through an event called Old Slaves Day, hosted by Southern Pines from 1934 to 1937 as the centerpiece of the Spring Blossom Festival, a multiday cultural showcase featuring a ceremony honoring former Union and Confederate soldiers. Regarding the inclusion of Old Slaves Day, the *Pilot* reported,

> The Negro is a branch of the human race peculiar in his character and his development and habit, intensely interesting in his peculiarities, of many exceedingly amiable characteristics, one of the most striking novelties of ethnology as compared with his white companion. To the man from the North he is a perennial wellspring of astonishment and mystery. His persistent good nature, his regard for white folks, his adaptability, his loyalty where loyalty is essential, his apparent shiftlessness at times, his quick wit, his musical ability, and many other traits make him one of the most valuable elements of life in the South. ("May" 1)

At the inaugural Old Slaves Day, three thousand spectators assembled in the downtown park for the morning session to witness the "registration" of eighty-six formerly enslaved people, the oldest being Mary Bass and Demus Taylor, both 106 years old. All of them were lined up on benches and chairs where they talked about their lives in slavery with the public. After a picnic provided by former slaveholders, the afternoon session opened with songs by the Shaw University Jubilee Singers. This was followed by the welcome address, storytelling by elderly gentlemen who recounted their experiences in slavery, dancing, singing, and fiddle and banjo picking contests. Keynote speakers included Black ministers Reverend William Cooper and Reverend George Goode, along with James Boyd and Bion Butler.

What Green thought about Old Slaves Day and Boyd's participation is not known. He would have heard about the event from visits to Southern Pines and from newspaper accounts. Some reports claimed that Black participants were lying about having been enslaved, including the editor of the *Greensboro News* who said, "If they had 80 old slaves down there, 75 of them must have come from Harlem, or Hollywood" (Williamson 6). This would have troubled Green whose support for racial justice was raising eyebrows, and Boyd being a party to such racist undertakings was certainly a divide between them. They had used Black people with their stories of enslavement to bolster their resort economy in an economic downturn. At any rate, the *Pilot* never again mentioned Boyd's name in association with Old Slaves Day. However, he remained a contributing editor along with others from the writing colony, and the newspaper continued to describe the event in racist terms.

Old Slaves Day was discontinued as older residents passed away and with the continuing economic downturn of the Great Depression. Over the years, some descendants have said the event wasn't offensive to them and they wished their family stories could have been recorded. They were aware local white leaders encouraged these gatherings as a tourist attraction and despite blatant racism, Black people helped plan the event—and the formerly enslaved participants, most of them living in poverty, are said to have appreciated the recognition. Roderick Brower says,

> If Old Slaves Day had been held for the purpose of maintaining history, it could have been wonderful. But as an extracurricular activity for folks to mock people their ancestors wrongly enslaved, to talk about those times as an entertainment—it sickens me. The fact that these elderly people felt good just to tell their story, even as a minstrel, shows their sadness and resolve. They had been trained to think they were less than anyone else.

There are sixteen doors leading into Weymouth, and it is said that Paul Green always came in through the kitchen entrance that the servants used, a gesture that made a strong impression on the Black people that worked at the house. Their reaction to events in the community is difficult to trace. Among the many workers, four were full-time residents: Thomas Wade, the butler; his wife, Lucy, a maid; Elizabeth W. Bell, also a maid; and Brower's great-uncle, Hilton Walker, the gardener. In 1982, Willa Mae Harrington, the niece of Thomas Wade, was interviewed for an oral history project. She said her family supported annexation but acknowledged uncertainty about the exclusion of Black leaders. Mrs. Harrington added that West Southern Pines wasn't a safe place because people from outside the community were coming there and committing crimes.

Around the time of the annexation, *Scribner's* magazine published "Bloodhound," a story by Boyd about an armed posse of white men running down a suspected thief with a bloodhound in "Jim Crowtown" (209). The dog leads them to a Black man whom they falsely accuse of stealing after ransacking his house without a warrant and threatening him with physical violence. The *Pilot* made a brief mention of the piece, reporting that it was based on the actual account of an incident in West Southern Pines. The story shines the light of day on the use of dogs as tools of oppression and on the limited concept of Black humanity held by many of those in Weymouth social circles.

Over the course of the 1930s Green's friendship with Boyd strengthened, helping to shape the Southern Pines author's recognition of social injustice. The two would get together and read aloud from each other's work. They would go to square dances with their wives and attend Black church services. Green started giving Boyd copies of his scripts and dedicated *Roll Sweet Chariot* to him, a 1934 play about Black American life in a small town.

At the height of the Depression, Green's work struck a powerful activist note with *Hymn to the Rising Sun*, his 1936 play about the brutality of chain gangs. This work was prompted in part by news Boyd brought to Green about convicts whose legs were amputated due to gangrene after their feet froze while locked in an unheated cell in the dead of winter. Green said tragedy was what he was after in the piece, since the lives he was characterizing were tragic. His hope was that drama would spark public outcry, and the chain gang would be abolished in North Carolina.

In 1937, *The American Mercury* magazine published "Civic Crisis," a satire by Boyd about a small-town policeman who could empathize with the troubles of a dog but not those of Black residents, as crime after crime is reported: a break-in, an attempted robbery, a knife fight. Likely the story was triggered by local attitudes toward Black people. Green wrote to congratulate his friend on the piece, saying, "Brother in arms, you have sure gone and done it. It's great. In fact, I am ready to say it's one of the subtlest, slickest, choicest pieces of American delineation of these and recent times" (Avery 280).

In a 1939 letter, Green shared his thoughts with Boyd during the lead-up to World War II, dreading the prospect of war but patriotic in the cause of freedom:

> Each morning's paper fills me with worse confusion and darkness. I can make no sense of the set up. Here tonight's paper glares at me "England and France will aid Franco" and so it goes with all the premiers and kings and dictators saying to one another "Go fuck yourself, for it's me and mine über alles (above all else)." I love this world, but it means too little unless I can love what men do to it and in it. But on! (Avery 300)

In 1941, Green collaborated with Richard Wright to write the Broadway stage adaptation of Wright's best-selling novel, *Native Son* (1940). In his story, Bigger Thomas, a Black youth in Chicago is seeking his identity in a world filled with systemic racism, and he mistakenly kills a white girl. Green invited Wright, a Black man with Communist sympathies, to Chapel Hill at the start of their work together. Because of segregation laws, Wright couldn't get a room at any Chapel Hill hotel, so he boarded with a nearby Black family. During his stay, Wright was threatened by a mob of white supremacists that included one of Green's cousins. They were angered by Wright's presence at a racially mixed party with white women, so they planned to hunt him down. Green calmed the mob down but spent the night outside Wright's boarding house in case they returned with guns and rope.

Green and Wright met again in New York while the Broadway production was already in rehearsal, but they had a serious disagreement over a single page of the script. They reached an impasse over the meaning of the crime depicted in Wright's story. Green felt that we controlled our destiny, while Wright felt that society determines what we become. Contrary to Green, Wright had determined for his protagonist to be a monster so that society might see how monstrous it is. Wright ultimately won out, Green's ending wasn't used, and their friendship fell apart.

Boyd surrendered foxhunting and writing novels in 1941 to organize a group of authors into the Free Company of Players, producing a series of radio dramas about the freedoms and rights that Americans must defend. Green contributed "A Start in Life," its setting a Black family's cabin and a nearby university. A father and son haul wood for a white professor. It's the son's first day of work, the boy barefoot in freezing weather because they can't afford shoes. The professor complains constantly about their work. When the Black men have trouble with their wagon, the professor takes control and drives the rig so hard a wheel falls off. The professor laughs and fires them. Returning home, the boy tells his mother he's crying because his father didn't push back against their harsh treatment. The mother holds her husband in her arms, stopping him from beating their son and returning to kill the professor.

Green's radio play reflects the attitude and behavior of Sandhills writing colony authors Katharine Ball Ripley and Bion Butler, and even Boyd to some degree. The white professor is self-entitled, condescending at best, and he thoughtlessly dashed the hopes and dreams of a Black family. This play comes at a time in Boyd's life when he is moving toward greater introspection. Green has been engaging him for years, providing him with copies of his scripts, sharing his urgent calling to affirm equality for everyone. The Free Company gave Boyd the opportunity to advance and amplify the voices of his activist colleagues and to brave the storm of ridicule himself.

The Free Company broadcasts reached nearly five million people each week, and provoked controversy from both the political right and left over its depictions of discrimination against Black Americans and immigrants. Seven months after the final program, Japan bombed Pearl Harbor and the nation plunged into war. In this time of war, upheaval, and loss, Boyd wrote to Green saying, "Nothing is left, on this earth at least, for us to believe in, except the spirit of those we know and love" (qtd. in Whisnant,

"Boyd's" 9). Such inner reflection informed most of Boyd's writing in his final years of life.

Boyd bought the *Pilot* in 1941, acquiring the nearly bankrupt weekly from his friend, Nelson Hyde, who had served as editor since the death of Bion Butler in 1935. Under Hyde's tenure, the paper had served as a "publicity agent" for the community, advancing economic interests while reporting on current happenings—church affairs, sewing circles, the comings and goings of esteemed community members—its editorials geared toward the limited interests of a small-town reader (Hyde).

Boyd transformed the *Pilot* into a progressive regional paper designed to foster a wider worldview. He favored civil rights for Black people and equal rights for women and advocated for free speech amid growing intolerance of dissent. In a 1942 editorial, he said we should remember that while men make war, they also create music and books, and if someone could compose the *Ninth Symphony* or write *Hamlet*, there was hope that someday we might discover how to use our "mighty powers" to shape a new world ("Our" 2).

While Boyd enjoyed his aristocratic life and found little fault with it, his ideas were democratic. Up until this time, he had never directly pushed back against the status quo in the same way Green did, opting instead for letting his stories shine a light on troubling aspects of his world. He had taken a "gradualist approach" to civil rights, which came to a head through a pair of articles written for the *Nation* in 1943, the first article by Boyd followed by a reply from Horace R. Cayton Jr., a well-known Black newspaperman.

In his article, "Strategy for Negroes," Boyd writes that there are two strategies open to Black leaders in their struggle for civil rights—gradualism or violence—and that it wasn't possible to follow both strategies simultaneously. He suggested that violence would erode white support for social justice and that efforts should be concentrated on the economic front where they would find greatest success. Boyd warned of the dangers of communist sympathies among Black intellectuals and of attacks on liberals, particularly those from the South, who had devoted themselves to fighting the "natural enemies" of Black people. He also cautioned the would-be activists saying, "Let him remember how slowly history moves and that all must accept responsibility for their part in it" ("Strategy" 887).

Boyd singled out author Richard Wright in his article under the heading "Wasted Assets," criticizing Wright's story "What You Don't Know Won't Hurt You," published by *Harper's Magazine* in 1942, about the accidental release of laboratory animals by a Black lab assistant who randomly puts them back in their cages to avoid detection. According to Boyd, "The story is marked by infantile glee at the triumph over white stupidity. Such glee is characteristic of an oppressed people's attitude toward its oppressors, but in a racial leader one would expect some recognition that faithfulness to his trust is an asset in the Negro's struggle" ("Strategy" 886).

In his reply to Boyd, titled "The Negro's Challenge," Horace Cayton pointed out that America's inaction on racial equality undermined democracy, and he equated the problems faced by Black Americans with the problems faced by people of color globally. According to Cayton, World War II opened the door to greater opportunities for Black people giving them a new sense of dignity and making them challenge segregation, particularly in a war being fought for freedom. He suggested that if violence erupted, it would likely be caused by an unwillingness to accept a change in the status of Black people, adding, "The Negro by refusing to accept gradualism may be helping America to save itself, helping to establish the new world order which must eventually come if Western civilization is not lost to fascist reaction" (12).

With his health in decline, Boyd spent the winter of 1943 living in New York to be near his doctor. On February 24, 1944, he went to Princeton University to give a lecture on the South as part of an "Americanization Course" for British army officers. He dined that evening with a group of soldiers. Shortly after midnight, they were sitting around laughing and talking, when in the middle of a story he suddenly fell forward and died from a cerebral hemorrhage. The news reached Weymouth the next morning, rippling out across the community where he had long been a part—his family, friends, and state suffering an irreparable loss.

Soon after his death, Boyd's final book, *Eighteen Poems*, was published. Paul Green wrote the introduction:

For twenty-five years I lived near James Boyd in North Carolina. I knew him well, took trips with him, sat many a night in his hospitable home and talked the dark away. . . . And as I knew him so did I love him. And long ago I said to myself that being a friend to him was one of the bright things of my life, and that nothing should ever happen to take that friendship away. And nothing did. (xiii)

Their relationship developed in spite of early ideological differences, leading Boyd to a broader perspective on race than he might otherwise have had. In 1952, his friendship with Green was mentioned in a review of a collection of his short stories that said, "They traveled the same country, heard the speech from the same people, saw the same humor and tragedy and the same beauty and bleakness in the landscape" (Norris 2). In his journey, Green helped him turn away from an all-encompassing atmosphere of racism.

"The Black Boys" is a poem included in *Eighteen Poems*, its context given in a 1943 editorial in the *Pilot* where he criticizes a strike at Baltimore's Sparrows Point Shipyard that began when Black workers were admitted to welding school: "There never has been any reason why a negro should not be allowed to earn a living according to his capacities. With a war on the case for using these capacities is stronger than ever. Especially since it is a war for freedom" ("Black" 2). In the last stanza of the poem Boyd writes,

Our sailors crowd the seas,
Our fliers sweep the sky,
But neither those nor these
Know whom they fight nor why
So long as knowledge mounts,
Through battles lost or won,
That in its true accounts
Our freedom is undone
Not by the foe in distant lands,
But by the black boys' empty hands.

Boyd's hope for a better world did not die with him. His wife, Katharine, went on publishing the *Pilot*, taking stands on the challenges of her day such as civil rights, labor relations, war, and the role of women in society. She encouraged businesses to hire minorities, saying it was a "moral issue," and she railed against police brutality toward civil rights marchers, comparing it to Nazism (Case). She issued a pointed warning about the danger of oil, chemical, and armament industries aided by powerful media, an alignment she called "straws in an evil wind," which must never be ignored ("Straws" 2). Over the years, she won many awards as a writer before selling her newspaper in 1968 to Sam Ragan, the first Poet Laureate of North Carolina. Through it all, she remained close to Green, who would ultimately help to sustain her family's legacy.

After Katherine Boyd passed away, Paul Green worked with others to save Weymouth, a rambling two-story southern colonial mansion with a double-portico central block featuring an ornate downstairs "great room" and flanking wings, set on pine-shaded grounds with extensive gardens, the perfect site for literary retreats and other cultural gatherings. This led to the establishment of Friends of Weymouth, a nonprofit corporation that purchased the property in 1979 to establish a cultural center. Since that time, more than six hundred authors have worked in the house through a writers-in-residence program, and the ancient stand of longleaf pines first spared from the axe by the Boyd family are part of the Weymouth Woods-Sandhills Nature Preserve, now the oldest remnant of a once ninety-million-acre forest that had spanned the Eastern Seaboard. Paul Green and James Boyd were both posthumously inducted into the North Carolina Literary Hall of Fame in 1995, a special room of Weymouth in what was once James Boyd's study, set aside to honor Tar Heel writers through the decades.

As friends, Paul Green and James Boyd shared so much of life, an unlikely pair who developed an extraordinary rapport. In terms of their legacy, Roderick Brower, as a servant's descendant, believes that Boyd could have done more to address racism in the 1920s and '30s, but he might have lost his livelihood, even his life, and many of his friends would have abandoned him. "Except for Paul Green," says Brower. "He was a wonderful man, unafraid to voice his opinions—a hero to me. Later in life, Boyd seems to have had a 'come to Jesus moment' when he realized his shortcomings and tried to make up for them."

Brower's words are a reminder of the work that lies ahead if we are to follow in Paul Green's footsteps, considering that residents of West Southern Pines are still fighting to improve their neighborhood. Economic segregation continues, since the relative affluence of Pinehurst and Southern Pines excludes both Black and white high-needs residents from community development funding by the state, creating an additional burden on schools and public services. A section of the neighborhood known as "Lost City" is completely encircled by Southern Pines but not part of the town, with existing state laws making it almost impossible to solve this problem. And even with a town task force focused on the area, the relationship between local government and the neighborhood remains challenging.

Love Is the Soul of Man

Back in the '90s, when I worked as a temp on the UNC campus in Chapel Hill, I would walk across Raleigh Road on my lunch hour and visit Paul Green's grave. I didn't grow up in North Carolina, so I knew only generally who he was: a classmate of my early writer crush Thomas Wolfe, an activist for liberal causes, the playwright for whom the theater on campus was named. I would visit his grave not only for the peace and the birdsong among old shade trees, but also for the words carved on stone:

PAUL GREEN

Teacher Dramatist Philosopher

ELIZABETH LAY GREEN

LOVE IS THE SOUL OF MAN

That last line got me.

I had been writing a novel and poems and stories, but lately I'd been thinking of giving up. I was paying bills. Putting one foot in front of the other. I was a writer whose budding hopes had faded. I was a wife who had lost the hope of a child through miscarriage.

But in my visits to those conjoined graves, I began to feel a strange affinity. They were speaking back to me, these married people who believed in philosophy, souls, and love. I imagined sitting at their dinner table, basking in writer talk. I pretended that if I'd just gotten to North Carolina a few years earlier, Paul Green might have been my mentor. I might have known what to do next to crawl out of my pit of despair.

I began to put small offerings on the gravestone: a stone, a leaf, a petal.

Though familiar entirely through imagination, this long dead couple began to belong to me.

Now I see that by imagining our affinity, I was practicing creativity again. By marking the seasons with seasonal gifts, I was marking the healing qualities of time.

One fall day, it occurred to me that I just didn't know what I was doing with my writing. A friend suggested graduate school. I applied. I got in. I gave notice. I left one last gold leaf on the pediment of Paul Green's grave and walked away to a new life.

Before I completed that graduate program, I received an offer to write a book about Virginia Dare, a name that, as a newcomer to the South, I had scarcely heard before — once, at a women's writers conference, then later in an eighth-grade history book I had edited. Knowing about Virginia Dare was a kind of secret handshake for real North Carolinians, the ones born and bred here — a little like knowing who Paul Green was.

By this time, I knew Green had been a mentor to Black writers. He was also a Pulitzer prize–winning playwright for an early drama exposing the plight of a Black man in the racist South. He was an activist against the death penalty. And remarkably, he and his wife had lived just up the road from me in Chatham County.

Now, with my assignment to write about Virginia Dare, Paul Green's writing life would converge with my own. As most born-and-raised North Carolinians know, Green had written and produced *The Lost Colony*, a play telling the story of Virginia Dare and her people, who were part of the first English settlement in the New World. Green's 1937 play was still in production on Roanoke Island, near the site of the settlement. On August 18, 1999, the anniversary of Virginia Dare's birth, I went to see it. I did not know then that the story of Virginia Dare, in legend, art, and Paul Green's play, would lead me into an awareness of the limits of white-centric American history, an awareness that laid the groundwork for my own advocacy work and to writing about systemic racism in my own fiction.

Everywhere they lived. Paul and Elizabeth Green loved working together in their gardens. Their last home, called Windy Oaks, is now a bed and breakfast in Chatham County, North Carolina. Photo courtesy of the Paul Green Foundation.

I hand over my ticket to the gatekeeper at the Waterside Theatre, the rustic outdoor amphitheater on the shore of the Albemarle Sound, and settle into my seat. The sun sets behind me, colors flare in the sky, and a breeze holds mosquitoes at bay. I look around. I am surrounded by families with young children. Notebook in hand for scribbling in the dark, I ask the man next to me if he has seen the play before. "Yes," he says, "as a kid."

"Was it good?" I ask.

"All I remember," he grins, "is a lot of Indian dancing and a big noise."

I write that down.

In the historic record, the story of the Roanoke colony is complex. It includes more than three voyages from England under three different English leaders. It includes the life stories of Manteo and Wanchese, two
Indigenous men who travel to England. It includes scientific discovery, the
first English paintings of the New World, its fish and people, and Native
dances. It includes the court of Queen Elizabeth I. It includes the Spanish
Armada. It includes the birth of Virginia Dare.

Paul Green somehow compresses all of these complexities into dramatic
highlights. The scenes move from London docks to a wilderness island;
from sword fights to hymns and folk songs; from formal dances in the
Queen's courts to rough huts and violent encounters. As is all too common
in first-contact stories, the violence starts with the English. Soldiers from
the second voyage, under Ralph Lane, ambush and kill Wingina, king of
a local tribe, making enemies for life. Manteo, unaccountably, remains a
friend to the English while Wanchese declares his allegiance to his tribe
and promises to avenge the death of their leader.

The Native dancing roles on that night in 1999 were performed by white
actors in body paint, as they had been since Paul Green's opening night in
1937. On the set, carved posts formed a circle, as in the famous John White
painting of a 1500s Native dance. And there is singing: gorgeous harmonic
English voices. At a peak moment, Virginia Dare is baptized, the first
English child born in America, a tiny icon of hope, named Virginia for
the new land the colonists claimed, which in turn had been named for the
Virgin Queen.

From this high point Paul Green's colony descends into chaos, and
Manteo is killed in a skirmish. The colonists suffer starvation and cold.
A Spanish ship is set to attack. The colonists fight among themselves, finally uniting under a new leader to march bravely into the dark wilderness,
carrying bags and baggage and sleeping children, away from the coming
threat. The brave mothers carrying their children, the brave fathers, the
chorus returning to song are not enough to wipe away the sad certainty of
their hopeless situation. It is a play that poses an enduring mystery: how
these English people in the New World disappeared, how their children
disappeared. Implied in the story is this: Manteo's people disappeared too.

I liked the play. I loved the music. The Queen's costume was resplendent. But the play hit home for me after the final scene: to get back to our cars, the audience followed a dimly lit winding trail of parents carrying bags and baggage and sleeping children through the dark forest.

I am reading *A Southern Life: Letters of Paul Green, 1916–1981*, a seven-hundred-plus-page record that reveals Green's creative struggles in equal measure with his staunch integrity in standing up for his beliefs: educational equity for people of color; mentorship for Black writers; defense of poor and vulnerable people; advocacy for those on death row. A surprising thread is kindness: even when he comes down like thunder on a letter writer, Green always ends with a salutation of respect. The letters are infused with warmth toward his students, colleagues, family, even his political adversaries, and as I turn pages, I am more brokenhearted than ever that I did not know him. But here, I do find insight into how his creative mind worked.

In one of the letters, Green discusses how *The Lost Colony* came to be written and produced. As a young man in college, he was haunted after visiting Roanoke Island by thoughts of the tragic first colonists. Then years later, he met up with two local businessmen on the island who had hopes of creating some kind of commercial celebration of the colony to boost the economy. Their thoughts, Green writes, included the "rather startling" idea of holding a Virginia Dare beauty contest, in lieu of which Green offered his interest in making a play (Avery 302).

"There was in all our minds the legend that she grew up to be a beautiful maiden and fell in love with Chief Manteo's son, married him and became the mother of a brave race that somehow evaporated into thin air," Green explains (Avery 302). This idea, taken from a popular romantic poem by Sallie Southall Cotten, was fiction, so Green turned away from that romance in his script, instead sticking to documented facts—Virginia Dare was born and baptized, and then she disappeared. He moved into fiction only so far as to carry her into the wilderness in her mother's arms. Green may not have known that there was in fact some historic documentation for the probability of intermarriage between English and Indigenous people. As far back as 1709, the reliably accurate explorer and writer John Lawson encountered Hatteras Indians on the Outer Banks, who eagerly explained the source of their gray eyes: "These tell us, that several of their Ancestors were white People and could talk in a Book [read] as we do" (69). This record could have provided justification for Green centering his play on a serious love match between a colonist and one of Manteo's people. (Green does include a comedic storyline about a lovesick tribal woman, "Agona," who attaches herself to "Old Tom," an English drunkard, but it's played for laughs.) But Green did not appear to know about Lawson's report. (UNC Press's first scholarly edition of Lawson's book was not published until 1966.) And perhaps he wanted to avoid raising the issue of miscegenation, still illegal in North Carolina at the time. Perhaps his financial backers would blanch.

What became of the real Virginia Dare, Green's tiny icon of hope for the future of English people in the New World? As Indigenous populations in the East diminished—through war, government policy, pestilence, and diaspora—nineteenth-century white artists and writers began to reinvent them in fiction and art. James Fenimore Cooper published *The Last of the Mohicans* in 1826. Longfellow published his epic poem *The Song of Hiawatha* in 1855. In the works of two nineteenth-century American women, one working in stone and one in epic poetry, Virginia Dare was reimagined as a beautiful Indian princess—a white one.

In 1859, the young American sculptor Louisa Lander created the *Virginia Dare Venus* in her studio in Rome. Carved of Carrara marble, Michelangelo's favored stone, and seemingly inspired by her visit to the British Museum in London, where she had viewed Roanoke Colony artist/Governor John White's seminude drawings of Indigenous women, the Venus shows an Anglo woman, half nude, in a classic Greek goddess pose, draped in fishnet, upper arms ornamented with pearl and shell bracelets, a heron companion beside her delicate feet.

After its creation in Rome, Lander's *Venus* had many surprising adventures. First came a shipwreck off the coast of Spain, then salvage and restoration, then a gallery fire in New York, then the death of a buyer midtransaction and reversion to the artist's possession for a respite in the artist's home in Washington, D.C. Even after it made its way to North Carolina years later (with the help of North Carolina poet and activist Sallie Southall Cotten), the *Venus* suffered vandalism in Raleigh, flood on the Outer Banks, even a short period of exile in Paul Green's backyard just up the road from me in Chatham County. With Green's assistance, the *Venus* finally found her home at the end of a shady copse in the Elizabethan Gardens on Roanoke Island, just through the woods from the Waterside Theatre. The statue quickly became part of the island ecosystem, pleasantly pale green with mold and shaded by live oaks draped with Spanish moss, ethereal as a wood nymph. Paul Green had chosen her placement in the Gardens, within earshot of the lapping waters of Albemarle Sound, a place where he had had a vision of young Virginia playing in the woods as a child.

In the late 1800s in Greenville, North Carolina, Sallie Southall Cotten was hatching her own vision of what happened to Virginia Dare. Inspired in part by Lander's *Venus*, in 1901 she published an epic poem: *The White Doe: The Fate of Virginia Dare, An Indian Tale*, seemingly crediting it to Indigenous sources. Like Lander's statue, Cotten's Virginia Dare fantasy depicts the grown-up Virginia as a white Indian princess. But here's an interesting twist. Lander's statue stands alone in her white marble purity, but Cotten's Virginia falls for a handsome young man of Manteo's tribe. Love connects across boundaries in this tale. But before the lovers can marry, a jealous shaman turns young Virginia into a white doe. Through complications involving two crossing arrows, the doe is both killed and transformed, turning back into a young woman lying in a pool of blood.

In this epic, Virginia is beautiful, pale-faced, worshipped, and admired—as "one of the developed races" and Manteo's people are "rude, untutored savages" (43). But in Cotten's preface she expresses a firm conviction that the English colonists "became part of a tribe of friendly Croatoan Indians, shared their wanderings, and intermarried with them" (xiv). There is a contradiction in Cotton's racial attitudes: white Virginia may be goddess-like and superior, but the salvation of her Lost Colony came through becoming Croatoan.

Like Paul Green and Sallie Cotten, when I came up against the vast chasm of missing facts while telling the Lost Colony story, I slid into fiction, but my scenes tended toward the dire. In one scene, a ragged group of English is kept in bondage by the Chowanoc chief. In another there's a desperate journey to Lumbee territory by Hatteras survivors, escaping the Tuscarora War and all that followed: "But now so many warring braves have traveled her people's secret paths, burning crops, stealing women; now so many English warriors, with their pale eyes and fine clothes and funny booted stride, have passed so close by" (Hudson 120). There is no happy or romantic ending written for this story.

To my great surprise, when *Searching for Virginia Dare* was published in 2002, it was well received. Like Paul Green's Lost Colony play, it gained an audience among visitors to the Outer Banks. And it also attracted invitations to speak to historical societies throughout the state, including those in Haw River, New Bern, and Murfreesboro; a chapter of the Daughters of the Confederacy in Durham; and the Virginia Dare chapter of the Daughters of the American Revolution in Kitty Hawk. As I started each talk, I always asked who in the audience had heard of Virginia Dare? The answer almost always came in this form: "The first white child born in America."

"Yes," I would gently alter the language, "the first English child born on American soil, part of Queen Elizabeth's colony in the New World." "First English child" was the language that I have since noticed Paul Green used in his letters; perhaps, like me, with his antennae out for racism, he was uncomfortable about how easily the differentiating phrase "white child" fell from the lips of Carolinians. What did Virginia Dare's whiteness signify to these North Carolinians? Was it a Southern habit of speech from a bygone era? I wondered, but I did not ask.

As I toured, another revelation occurred. Town by town, season by season, I began to see signs for local powwows. There was a new powwow in Manteo. There was one on Hatteras. There was one just up the road from me, in Mebane. The Lumbee were not the only eastern nation of Native people who were still here.

I continued to visit Green's play on Roanoke Island many times, saw the cast, and heard the lines change over the years. At Elizabethan Gardens, in the lecture hall and, informally, at the foot of Lander's *Virginia Dare Venus*, I would tell tourists the story of her fascinating misadventures. Lingering late with her one summer afternoon, I heard drumming through the woods. It was, of course, white actors rehearsing for Green's play.

––––––––––––––––

In 2006 I took down my website SearchingforVirginiaDare.com and let the URL go, looking to save some money. Shortly after, I discovered "V-Dare .com," a website advocating virulent anti-immigrant-of-color policies, insisting that the United States was born in purity and whiteness, and claiming Virginia Dare as its icon of white supremacy. My god, I thought, my beloved sister-in-law is an immigrant and a person of color. I'm an advocate for Black history in my community. What if V-Dare was absorbing all Virginia Dare–related URLs, including my former one, and besmirching the name of the historical figure I'd been promoting? I frantically called my web hosting site to reclaim the URL I'd used for my book, but someone had bought it. It took four years to reclaim it. I avoided studying the group or visiting the website, sure that if I ignored it, it would go away. But it didn't go away.

In 2016, the writer Andrew Lawler contacted me. "I understand you're the expert on Virginia Dare," he said. "I'd like to come and interview you for my book." Lawler asked me what I knew about Virginia Dare being associated with white supremacists. I told him about my URL scare. He told me about more. In his book, *The Secret Token*, he devotes a chapter to Virginia Dare and multiple pages to the history of southerners using her image to promote white purity and supremacy. I was appalled at what I learned. Had I unwittingly promoted an icon of white supremacy? Had Virginia Dare been a dog whistle for "V-Dare" thinking all along? Was I so naive because I wasn't from the South? I wasn't giving Virginia Dare talks any more, but it festered in the back of my mind.

In 2021 I got the chance to speak out against white supremacy's coopting of the Virginia Dare legend. The Discovery Channel was putting together a documentary about some new archeological research on Hatteras Island, where British archeologist Mark Horton and Hatteras researcher Scott

Dawson had a new dig near the site of Croatoan Village. In previous digs in the area, they had found Indigenous midden and English artifacts in separate layers, then commingled in the sandy soil. In Dawson's *The Lost Colony and Hatteras Island*, he concluded that after John White left his colonists behind, Native people and English of the Roanoke colony era lived in settlements side by side on Hatteras Island, then eventually together, making a brave new tribe of mixed-race people. Dawson is not a fan of Paul Green's play. "The story" of the Lost Colony, he wrote, "has been buried in mythology and fiction stemming from the popular play of the same name" (18). He goes on to say that his own work has shown that the play's original ending, which promotes the idea that no one knows where the colonists went, is simply fiction. Instead, he says, his work has shown that "men, women, and children from two different worlds became one family. . . . [T]hey were the first assimilators, the first cross-cultural, the first cross-race family in America" (65).

Like Dawson's vision, Paul Green's original concept for a love story between an English girl born in the New World and one of Manteo's people has always made perfect sense to me, romanticized though it may be. John Lawson's reliable 1709 report corroborated the story that English ancestry was claimed by Hatteras people. Sallie Cotten's epic poem stops a hair shy of family-making; Lander's *Venus* is coolly European in expression, but very much Native in ornament. There may be appropriation in these visions, but also an urge to converge English America's fate with that of Native people, as in Dawson's vision.

To my great surprise, the producer of the upcoming documentary wanted to include me in his film. "We heard you were an expert on Virginia Dare," he said, flatteringly. He wanted me to talk about the *Virginia Dare Venus*, its fascinating history, and oh, by the way, what about Virginia Dare and white supremacy? "It will be cinema verité," he said. "Handheld cameras. Walking and talking down the path in Elizabethan Gardens. A casual conversation." I wasn't sure how to talk about white supremacy without getting visibly upset about the appropriation of Virginia Dare's name to promote it. What if I choked? What if I forgot everything I ever knew as I walked down the shaded green paths of Elizabethan Gardens? What if I said the wrong thing? What if even talking about Virginia Dare would identify me as white supremacist to people who didn't know me? But this was my chance to speak up. I said yes.

To prepare, I went back to primary sources. This scenario in John White's log caught my eye: on July 30, 1587, twenty of White's men landed on Croatoan (known now as Hatteras Island), hoping to find friends among Manteo's people after the disastrous violence of the previous year's encounters. The governor reported that he wished "to renew our olde friendshippe with them." At first Manteo's people made to fight, then run away, but when Manteo (with White's party now) called to his people in their language, they dropped weapons and "some of them came unto us, embracing and entertaining us friendly" but asking White's men to not steal their food. White answered, "Our coming was onely [*sic*] to renew the olde love, that was between us, and them, at the first, and to live with them as brethren, and friends" (2: 526). A feast ensued. This may have been the first and perhaps the only time in English New World colonization that honest chastisement by Native people was followed by declarations of love and brotherhood by the English. Though of course this report was from an English source, it rings true to me, as White duly reported Manteo's scolding. That was something I wanted to talk about for the documentary.

In my room at the Heart of Manteo Motor Lodge, just next door to the new Peruvian chicken place, it's a chill December early morning. I put on my slimming black suit jacket, jeans, and black boots. My hair is moussed, and I'm jacked up on two cups of motel coffee. I didn't sleep much last night. I'm still practicing my answers to the ten most likely questions I figure Mark Horton will ask. The one question that I'm pretty sure he will ask is "Did you know Virginia Dare is associated with white supremacy?"

Yes. Yes, I knew. I have pretended not to know for years. Now there will be no pretending.

I arrive at the Elizabethan Gardens and find the crew hustling to find a workaround for enormous and jarring Christmas decorations placed alongside the winding forest paths, not the right mood for history talk at all. The sound tech fits me with a mic, cord slipped under my shirt. Mark Horton comes to greet me. He's wearing a puffy vest against the chill with a friendly grin on his face. He leads me to the familiar green path that ends at Virginia Dare. And there she is, same live oak overhead, same Spanish moss. But something is different.

They have washed off the lovely green patina from the statue, the camouflage that made her seem a romantic spirit hovering in the live oak forest by the sound. Virginia Dare is white. White, white, glow-in-the-dark white, a torch of whiteness in Carrara marble. Oh, dear god. She is so white.

In a matter of minutes, I navigate the easy questions, cinema verité-style, the flattering ones about how I am an expert on Virginia Dare, the practiced ones about how the statue ended up here. I know what's coming next. I know because I can sense a cameraman easing in from the right, in my peripheral vision. Closer. Closer. I've been told the worst thing to do on camera is to flick your eyes away. But I can't help it. He's really crowding in. He's practically at my shoulder. I know the question is coming. Mark Horton leans in, his expression intense. I flick my eyes.

"What do you say to white supremacists who use Virginia Dare to stand for white purity?" he says.

"It's ludicrous," I reply, suddenly hot under the collar. "If the colonists survived, if Virginia Dare survived, it was by joining forces, making families, with Manteo's people."

And they've got their shot. I can breathe again.

———————

My imaginary mentor has been haunting me for years. I see that now. Paul Green led me to take the risk of becoming a full-time writer. He led me to Virginia Dare. Virginia Dare led me to a fuller understanding of the South, of the complex history of southern Indigenous people, of the subtle racism in white-centered depictions of history, including those in Paul Green's popular play. But in the last few years, The Lost Colony has undergone a sea change. Living Indigenous people, the center of John White's fascinating paintings, the center of conflict and powerful transformations in the story, have come front and center.

In 1939, when advising CBS on music to use for its Lost Colony play broadcast, Green wrote, "You may wish to have some Indian music" (Avery

309), then recommended a song by North Carolina classical composer and folk music expert, Lamar Stringfield, a white man.

Though this suggestion might seem tone deaf by present standards, it is important to note that Indigenous people were not strangers to Green. When he was young, a small group of Coharie people (known to Green as "Croatans") lived near his family's farm in Harnett County. His knowledge of Robeson County's Lumbee nation had inspired his 1920 student production, *Last of the Lowries*. In 1960, when Lumbee children were barred from attending high school in Dunn, North Carolina, Green wrote an impassioned letter of support for their cause and helped raise funds so they could board in private homes and attend schools in other cities.

Yet it did not seem to occur to Green to consult living tribal people in the production of this play or its music, perhaps because all the Native people he knew were struggling to feed and house and educate themselves with no time for such frivolities as plays, perhaps because the singing and dance traditions of the Native people he knew had long since been dissipated by the crushing blows of poverty and diaspora. Perhaps those traditions had long since gone underground, and even educated white men such as Green knew little of them.

Over years, Native folk have come to Manteo to see *The Lost Colony* for themselves, and they noticed — the dances were wrong, the clothing and Indigenous ornaments were wrong, the speaking lines of Wanchese and Manteo were TV-Tonto pidgin English. The Indians weren't Indians at all. They were white people in red body paint.

Although the play has been revised many times over the years — by Paul Green as well as by the show's many directors — for more than seven decades, no one seemed to consider casting Native American roles with Native actors, except for a few extras. After all, this was a play about the English people who disappeared.

In 2020, in the era of Black Lives Matter, after an online petition protesting the "redface" practices in the play and the lack of Native input, the board chair and director of *The Lost Colony* reached out to local Lumbee leaders (the Lumbee being the largest Indigenous nation in North Carolina, and one whose identity has been historically tied to Croatoan people), asking them to help reimagine the play and find ways to include Indigenous people and history. That season the show was shut down by COVID, giving plenty of time for this work. By 2021, the director had cast twelve members from four tribes to take on Native dances and other roles.

A Lumbee woman, Kayla Oxendine, took the narrator role played in the past by a white man cast as a scholar. Another dramatic shift was the addition of puppets — owls, fish, bear, wolves, and deer — all essential creatures in local ecology and Native lore. Manteo's English became more standard, lines of Algonquin dialogue were included, and a Native blessing ceremony set the season running. But Indigenous cast members often felt out of place in the town of Manteo. There was an uncomfortable encounter with white locals in a laundromat. In a different incident, a local policeman, called to check on crew safety, instead threatened to use his Taser. The pay was dismal, the quarters cramped. But with the addition of these brave new cast members, Paul Green's play was transformed.

When the next season started, I got the opportunity to see it.

My cousin Leslie is hosting a cousin reunion on the Outer Banks — a new tradition for my northern relations — and we're making plans in a group text. After we all decide who is bringing food for the first night — me, barbecue — I text, "Do you want me to get tickets to The Lost Colony?" They've heard me talk about it. They all text yes. I'm finally going to Paul Green's play the way people born in North Carolina see it — with family.

My brother calls to tell me he wants to come a few days early to explore eastern North Carolina. What town should he and his wife stay in? I mention a few. And where's a good hotel? I mention a few. "Will they stare at us?" he says, protective of his wife, with her brown skin and Brazilian accent. I find myself shocked to be called into service as a modern-day "Green Book" guide to safe places in my new home state. But maybe he's right to be concerned. I try to think. "Manteo's good," I tell him. "They're used to tourists."

But then I wonder.

I'm taking a little break on my way to the cousin reunion to visit old haunts in downtown Manteo, stroll along the waterfront, listen to halyards clanging, watch people. Tourists, young kids, Black and Hispanic families picnic and play in shorts and tee shirts printed with slogans, modern American regalia. There's a crowd of what may be Amish people (women in long skirts and small hats) waiting to get on a tour boat. It seems that today, on this fine breezy afternoon by Albemarle Sound, Manteo village has served up a vision of friendly American diversity just for me. I stop at Poor Richard's, the local sandwich shop and pub where I've been known to have a beer and badger visitors with my perpetual question: *What do you think happened to Virginia Dare?*

I take my "Rockfish Wrap" outside to the covered deck. Across from me are three young men, joking and laughing, one with a man bun, one with long hair. One starts singing along with the piped-in '80s rock music. Nice voice. Others chime in. Maybe they're a band.

I'm getting ready to go. Enjoying their energy, I decide to break in. "You have nice voices. Are you in a band?"

"No," one of them says. The one with the man bun adds, "But we are in the entertainment business." He grins, a sparkle in his eye.

I get it. "Oh!" I exclaim. "You're in *The Lost Colony*!"

They laugh at my obvious delight. I explain that they are the reason I've come: to see the transformation Indigenous people have made in Paul Green's longest-running outdoor drama.

One explains that he is Pima, from Arizona. Another says he's Lumbee.

I tell them I'll look for them in the play.

Later that week, my siblings and cousins are all lined up, Row D, center section, COVID masks on. The sky glows deep blue over Albemarle Sound behind the stage. No clouds tonight. No mosquitoes. Perfect.

The Storyteller in Native dress walks out of darkness to the light at the front of the stage. She tells a new story, a story of the animals who lived here, sea turtle, fish, deer, bear. She tells the story of Turtle Island, the creation story of how the world was built on the back of a turtle. And there's something else—who are these people with sticks walking around? But then I see. These are the puppets I've heard about. The sticks are animal shapes. The shapes have eyes that glow. They come alive. The world is made of animals, fish, and Native people.

The Storyteller tells of the things that do not change. Weather, ocean, wind. And she tells of the day everything changed. The day the English came.

Paul Green's play has been shifted on its axis. Here's the court of Queen Elizabeth I, the doughty Eleanor Dare, arguing for women to come to the New World. But when Sir Walter Raleigh takes the stage, he is a handsome Black man. Here's the common farmer John Borden becoming a leader and the governor/artist/grandfather John White. But the story of the English newcomers now sits within a broader frame—the Outer Banks, the wild things, and Native people. All of which were here, in what is now North Carolina, in the beginning, but not on this stage until now.

When Manteo strides on stage, I recognize him. He's my new Lumbee friend from Poor Richard's Sandwich Shop. Another strides on stage as Wanchese. He's the Pima man I met.

In this play's storyline, Manteo is a constant friend and advisor to the colony. Green's silly, adoring Agona, the lovesick servant of Old Tom, has become a pretty, sweet partner. Other Native women and children share the stage with other colonists, helping repair fishnets, haul water. John White gets a scene where he sketches Manteo and Wanchese, asks Manteo for their names. The value of an artist on such a voyage becomes transparent: artists make a common language.

Chief Wingina arrives, a giant of a man, played by Cam Bryant, a Lumbee. What used to be a "loud noise"—the shooting of Wingina by Ralph Lane—has shifted into a metaphoric scene. Lane's soldiers become wolves, Wingina's spirit rises as a giant owl.

In the end, Manteo lives. He leads the colonists into the forest, fist raised, heading to Croatoan, his home village on Hatteras Island. They are not lost at all. They know exactly where they're going. It is the place where Scott Dawson and Mark Horton are digging up sword hilts and Elizabethan buttons along with turtle-shell and oyster-shell midden, in communities at first separated, then merged, then one. The place where Manteo's people and John White's men pledged renewed friendship, then feasted.

And what if the abandoned colonists and Manteo's people did survive at Croatoan, fall in love with each other, bear a brave new tribe of Americans? If Paul Green were alive today, I think he would be delighted that his play has been transformed in a way that celebrates a broader, more inclusive view of history. I imagine sitting with him at his dining room table at Windy Oaks, listening as he hatches a new play—or coaches a Hatteras or Lumbee writer to write one—a play about a Croatoan village where a young English girl grew up to marry a man of Manteo's tribe, affirming the surprising promise of a new world founded in love as well as violence.

Living My Native Past in the Present

The night has beckoned me here to this amphitheater as a specta-tor of the longest-running outdoor drama, Paul Green's *The Lost Colony*. Rain clouds hover against the sky, offering cool crisp air on a summer's evening. The atmosphere is clear and inviting. The tar-top path meanders into rows of stadium seating. The set glows, as if beaming with pride at the birth of this acculturation. The crowd is not large, and I find solace in that. It is a mixed crowd: those who view the storyline as past tense and those who feel it in the present. Because there are fewer people here tonight, a presence of peace swaddles me and the meaning of this play is able to rest gently against my soul.

Taking a seat, I am excited to be among my people as each character breathes life into this history. The characters of this drama are my people, the people of the Lumbee, are the people of the pine, people of the dark waters, rich with tannins, that lap against the knees of cypress trees. *My* people are the survivors of tribes whose cultures and rituals intertwined with the English colonizers who are being portrayed here. My people are part of the history put into motion long before "CRO" was carved into a tree. And on this night, my people live to tell the story of how we came to thrive along the present-day Lumber River.

Having grown up in Johnston County, North Carolina, not so far re-moved from my own community of Natives, though just far enough to feel ostracized both in the place where I lived and from the home that I longed for, I feel the palpable connection between the characters on the stage and the observers. It took many years before the painted red face no longer suited this play's script. It has previously been a disappointment to look at the cast and not see a face reflecting my own. The face of my people matters.

In her seventies and a member of the Snipe Clan of the Kahtehnuaka Tuscarora people, actor Kat Littleturtle performs in *The Lost Colony* in the new role of "The Storyteller." Originally the play's narrator was performed by a white male actor described in the script as "The Historian." For the first time, in the eighty-fourth season of the play, the production cast eleven American Indians from tribes across the region. Members of the Native community continue to provide historically accurate costuming, choreography, props, and musical instrumentation for the production. Photo courtesy of Cindy McEnery Photography.

Change has come. Native actors now portray the Native characters. Now, I see my own face and hear my own voice as the story pulses through my veins. I am Lumbee, a descendent of the Croatoan peoples. My DNA emerges from these lines, scenes, and monologues. I am more than an observer. It is now my face the observer sees, my voice the observer hears, and it is my story being shared. Watching the story unfold feels like triumph. I am joyful seeing my Native people cast as the ancestors who fought against toil and trouble. Each is as familiar as my mother's rocking when she caressed me against her bosom, humming songs of comfort in the soft light of the moon. My people represent me, and each face is glorious. My people, the descendants of this history, shatter the boundaries of representation.

This performance is not about a colony lost in history, but rather one that was birthed beneath this sky and of these estuaries, inscribing a heritage of its own. Natives and settlers forging rapport and interrelation. This account gives rise to the opportunity to thwart misrepresentation with heartbeats that keep time with our sacred drum. This is an account that raises our fists against red face and embraces the raw reality of "we are still here." *We are still here.*

Paul Green's *The Lost Colony* is a story of my people. The story of who we are intertwines like needles of longleaf pine with the fabric of English colonists, our histories stitched together to create panels of resilience, affability, and fortitude. There is not just one side to this story. One cannot exist without the other. One cannot be represented without the other.

My people were cultivated from the very grains of this sand, harvested, and replanted in soil as red as our souls. The breath of my people filled the lungs of this narrative. The heart still beats with the rhythm of the drum. Every footstep continues to stir up the dust of our ancestors. The strength of our men remains as tall as the trees, and the hum of our mothers continue to beckon in the still of the night. This story, one of an English colony mingled among the Natives of this land, is certainly not lost on me. It touches my soul.

Epilogue

Paul Green, "Deeply Haunted" Writer/Activist

"Who has seen *The Lost Colony* in Manteo?" That's the question I ask when students don't recognize the name Paul Green. "He's the playwright who wrote it and, with it, created the symphonic drama genre," I tell them. This is what I learned about Paul Green upon first moving to North Carolina, but then I was asked to complete a Green biography found after the author, James R. Spence, had died, and from the archival research I did for that project emerged one, two, three more research projects for myself, as well as several for the *North Carolina Literary Review*. "How is it that I did not read this writer when I was in graduate school?" I asked myself.

As Georgann Eubanks reminds us toward the end of her extensive coverage of the writer's life in letters, Green has left behind many portals into understanding his work and its role in his civic mission. Through his journals, extensive correspondence, and tape-recorded interviews, we can observe his ever-evolving social conscience and conscientiousness. He was often self-examining: "Why didn't I ask him to call me Paul?" he asked repeatedly when thinking back on his collaboration with the young Richard Wright. Wright respectfully called the senior writer "Mr. Green" throughout their relationship, even as Green called Wright "Dick." Today, few with any literary acumen have never heard of Richard Wright, author of *Native Son*, while the same cannot be said for Paul Green, despite his much larger oeuvre. What I heard in Green's question was a man discomforted by his younger, patronizing self; and, now an older man, he was willing to share that discomfort with his interviewers. And that is the Paul Green I am drawn to: a very human philosopher—that is, a flawed man who struggled to be a better man. Admired for his advocacy for the oppressed, Green not only recognized his own unconscious biases, he also was willing to ponder them before a witness. Ever the professor, perhaps he viewed such occasions during an interview as teaching moments.

My projects over the years, both through my own writing about Green and publishing writing by and about him in the *North Carolina Literary Review*, have endeavored to call attention back to this neglected writer, to appreciate, for example, how his writing complemented his social activism, as Mike Wiley and Lynden Harris explore in their discussions of Green's *Hymn to the Rising Sun*. Like Ian Finley, who tells us in his essay about how he came to write the play *Native* about Green's collaboration with Wright, I am drawn to the professor playwright who desegregated the UNC campus by bringing Black writers like Richard Wright to campus but then, in retrospect, questioned whether he went far enough rather than flattering himself for being more open-minded than those who were appalled by Wright's presence. Isn't it fitting that Paul Green would inspire a play (and now a film, inspired by Finley's play)? And with so much of his life recorded in journals, correspondence, and interviews, Finley had much material to draw from. Finley's play, like Green's, encourages discussions about the most difficult subjects, and such discussions are still needed.

Bringing Green's play *The House of Connelly* back into print to use in the classroom illuminated for me how drama is a unique genre in that it is ever evolving from production to production. With this play, and with his obsessive tinkering with other works as they were produced and reproduced, Green revealed his open mind. He would rethink, reconsider, and revise, again and again. And I believe he would be fine with others doing so as his dramatic works live on—most recently, as Synora Cummings and Marjorie Hudson write about, with the annual adjustments and particularly the most recent casting changes to *The Lost Colony*.

Eubanks describes the essays in this volume as "frank reflections on Green's work and relationships . . . meant to launch new conversations about a man who was seen as progressive, even radical, in his time." In her discussion of Green's one-act play *White Dresses*, Kathryn Hunter-Williams surmises that "Green wanted to push society into a conversation on the subject [of miscegenation]," but she, like several of the other writers in their essays, is deeply troubled by the supposedly progressive playwright's employment of stereotypical (and racist) tropes in his descriptions of the African American characters and in stage directions that seem to reflect innate prejudices in spite of his activism for civil rights. Agreeing with the observations of both Hunter-Williams and Jim Grimsley, who provides here a long-overdue candid reading of Green's Pulitzer Prize play *In Abraham's Bosom*, as well as a critical reading of *The House of Connelly*, I find myself better understanding the hesitancy to revive Green's plays when, as Hunter-Williams notes, there are other plays of the same period to choose from, ones that deserved but never got the kind of audience Green once had.

Grimsley recognizes Green's work as "transformative," his motives as "good" but not enough. He describes the playwright "as a man who had liberal ideas about Black oppression but also the baggage of unrecognized racism. As we all do." A distinction one might suggest about Green is that he does seem to have intuited his own innate prejudices—and was troubled by that self-awareness. It also may be why, as Jill McCorkle observes, he does not judge in his writing. Some may want more judgment against some of his villains, McCorkle says, but she argues that in simply reporting what he experienced, he "puts his readers in the position of witness. We are left to our own realizations and conclusions. We have seen and heard what so many have chosen *not* to see or acknowledge in those times and in our own."

McCorkle acknowledges that it is "impossible for some of [Green's] work to find a comfortable place in today's culture," but notes that even this work examines "right and wrong," that Green "recognize[d] injustice and went forward in his adult life trying to shine a light on it." She suggests that "Green was also deeply haunted . . . by those who witnessed, knew better, and did nothing." He wondered, she proposes, "Did their lack of action mean they shared the hatred?" He may have shared some of the innate prejudices, which also haunted him, as I've noted, but his reputation as liberal-minded, for his time, is supported by his activism. As Wiley and Harris discuss in their essays, he used his influence and his writing to seek retribution and justice, to give one example, for the two convicts whose abuse while in state custody led to the amputation of their limbs. Not only did Green threaten the North Carolina governor with calling in national press to cover their story if nothing was done, but then he wrote the play

Hymn to the Rising Sun, inspired by this injustice, thus recording for posterity the existence of a penal system that allows such abuse of prisoners. If you can't stop an injustice from occurring, Harris suggests, be a witness to it, as Paul Green was, rather than just turning away.

Ray Owen explores how Green became an example both in his activities and in his writing for his friend and fellow writer, James Boyd, tracing Boyd's development from writing in the tradition of plantation literature to joining Green's civil rights activism not only in his writing but in his community. Boyd is a writer whose work may no longer resonate for many, but his role (with Green) of developing the communal spirit among North Carolina writers who gathered in Southern Pines helped establish an early foundation for the community of writers we have today — who still gather at his estate. Both writers would be comforted to know that Jill McCorkle is leading among the most active state chapters of Writers for Democratic Action, that Mike Wiley regularly calls writers and arts advocates to action, that Lynden Harris brings underrepresented communities' stories to the stage with Hidden Voices. Marjorie Hudson notes how even though Green had passed on before she moved to North Carolina, she has long considered him a mentor.

As Green inspired Boyd to be more liberal-minded, so too does he continue to be inspirational to writers, and his work can still be inspirational. Phillip Shabazz reads the Green short story "Education South" and writes a letter to the deceased author, in lieu of the conversation he wishes they could have about the dead Black son in the story. Moving the young man from the margins of Green's story to a centerpiece of his own poem, Shabazz relates Green's story to the seemingly endless string of killings of young Black men and women by police officers, which gave birth to the Black Lives Matter movement in our time. (One feels certain Green would have joined the marches.)

Or, as Synora Cummings's reaction to the 2023 production of *The Lost Colony* implies, you might have to update Green's work to remove distractions from his advocacy of a true democracy for all Americans. For example, invite Native experts to the set and stage of *The Lost Colony* to bring authenticity to the roles Green included for the Native Americans in his play. Or, as Debra Kaufman did with Green's *Johnny Johnson*, diversify the cast to remind us that it is a play about the horror of *war*, not just World War I, and thus it is a play for all peoples and cultures. Remove distractions from that message, as Kaufman's revision does, and you have a play that will continue to resonate.

I appreciate all of these writers who have taken time to re-view North Carolina's preeminent playwright Paul Green. They share admiration for him even as their respective lenses focus candidly on flaws in the man and his work. Green had much to be proud of, but he knew he was still a work in progress. As we all are, to echo Grimsley. And the thing about Green's genre of choice, drama, is that it can more easily be adapted for the audience and needs of the day, even as it remains true to the playwright's intentions. We need only look to *The House of Connelly* for evidence of that. The Group Theatre asked for a new ending. Green gave them what they asked for, but both endings show that change must come to the South. Status quo is a death knell.

Following the ReGroup Theatre's production of *The House of Connelly* in New York in 2014 and after the performance of Ian Finley's play *Native* in Greenville, North Carolina, I participated in conversations with the audience about the tough issues addressed in these plays. Conversations about race are often discomforting, as Finley's play about Paul Green and Richard Wright hashing out their differences shows us, but still we must have these conversations, even or especially if they will help us to recognize and address our own biases and prejudices.

REFERENCES

Eubanks, Foreword

Warren, Marsha White, ed. *A Glimpse of Paul Green*. Paul Green Foundation, 1995.

McCorkle, "Bearing Witness"

Barnes, Billy E. Interview with Paul Green. Southern Oral History Program Collection, Southern Historical Collection. Wilson Library, University of North Carolina at Chapel Hill, 1975.

Cecelski, David. "The Red Shirts in Lumberton, N.C., 1900." *David Cecelski: New Writing, Collected Essays, Latest Discoveries*. 24 June 2021. https://david cecelski.com/2021/06/24/the-red-shirts-in-lumberton-n-c-1900/.

Green, Paul. *Home to My Valley*. Chapel Hill: University of North Carolina Press, 1970.

Morton, Brian. "Virginia Woolf? Snob! Richard Wright? Sexist! Dostoyevsky? Anti-Semite!" *New York Times*, 8 Jan. 2019.

Spence, James R. *Watering the Sahara: Recollections of Paul Green from 1894 to 1937*. Ed. Margaret D. Bauer. Office of Archives and History, North Carolina Department of Cultural Resources, 2008.

Wynn, Rhoda. Interview with Paul Green. Southern Oral History Program Collection, Southern Historical Collection. Wilson Library, University of North Carolina at Chapel Hill, 1975.

Hunter-Williams, "The Limits of the White Gaze"

Green, Paul. "A Consideration of Some Aspects of Negro Life in North Carolina." In *Lonesome Road: Six Plays for the Negro Theatre*, xx. New York: McBride, 1926.

———. *The House of Connelly: A Drama of the Old South and the New, in Two Acts* (1931). In *Paul Green's The House of Connelly: A Critical Edition*, ed. Margaret D. Bauer, 9–105. Jefferson, NC: McFarland, 2014.

———. *White Dresses: A Tragedy of Negro Life*. In *Five Plays of the South*, 291–307. New York: Hill and Wang, 1963.

Grimsley, "Comfortable and Uncomfortable Aspects"

Green, Paul. "Challenge to Citizenship." In *Drama and the Weather: Some Notes and Papers on Life and the Theatre*, 118–139. New York: Samuel French, 1958.
———. *The House of Connelly: A Drama of the Old South and the New, in Two Acts* (1931). In *Paul Green's The House of Connelly: A Critical Edition*, ed. Margaret D. Bauer, 9–105. Jefferson, NC: McFarland, 2014.
———. *In Abraham's Bosom: The Biography of a Negro in Seven Scenes*. London: George Allen and Unwin, 1929.

Wiley, "Stepping Over the Line"

Blackmon, Douglas A. *Slavery by Another Name: The Re-Enslavement of Black Americans from the Civil War to World War II*. New York: Doubleday, 2008.
Bryant, Erica. "Government Can't Say How Many People Die in U.S. Jails and Prisons." *Vera Institute of Justice*, 16 March 2022. https://www.vera.org/news/government-cant-say-how-many-people-die-in-u-s-jails-and-prisons.
Green, Paul. *Hymn to the Rising Sun: A Play in One Act* (1936). In *Five Plays of the South*, 179–204. New York: Hill and Wang, 1963.
———. *This Body the Earth*. New York: Harper, 1935.
Griffiths, Alison. *Carceral Fantasies: Cinema and Prison in Early Twentieth-Century America*. New York: Columbia University Press, 2016.
Hall, Jacquelyn Dowd. Interview with Paul Green. Southern Oral History Program Collection, Southern Historical Collection. Wilson Library, University of North Carolina at Chapel Hill, 1975.
Henderson, Lisa Y. "Negroes to Receive Lifetime Pension for Amputated Feet." *Black Wide-Awake*. 15 Oct. 2021. https://afamwilsonnc.com/2021/10/15/negroes-to-receive-lifetime-pension-for-amputated-feet/.
Wynn, Rhoda. Interview with Paul Green. Southern Oral History Program Collection, Southern Historical Collection. Wilson Library, University of North Carolina at Chapel Hill, 1974.

Harris, "Leaning Toward the Life"

Avery, Laurence G., ed. *A Southern Life: Letters of Paul Green, 1916–1981*. Chapel Hill: University of North Carolina Press, 1994.
Fischer, Heinz-Dietrich. "1927 Award." *Outstanding Broadway Dramas and Comedies: Pulitzer Prize–Winning Theater Productions*. Münster: LIT Verlag, 2013.
Green, Paul. *In Abraham's Bosom: The Biography of a Negro in Seven Scenes*. London: George Allen and Unwin, 1929.

Hall, Jacquelyn Dowd. Interview with Paul Green. Southern Oral History Program Collection, Southern Historical Collection. Wilson Library, University of North Carolina at Chapel Hill, 1975.

Ladd, Susan. "Paul Green: A Voice for Humanity." *Greensboro News & Record*, 5 March 1994.

"Paul Green: Fort Raleigh National Historic Site." National Park Service, 14 Sept. 2017, https://www.nps.gov/people/paulgreen.htm.

"Price of Progress." *Time*, 22 July 1935: 16.

Finley, "Problems of the Hero"

Avery, Laurence G., ed. *A Southern Life: Letters of Paul Green, 1916–1981*. Chapel Hill: University of North Carolina Press, 1994.

Baldwin, James. "Many Thousands Gone." In *Notes of a Native Son*. Boston: Beacon, 1955.

Bauer, Margaret D. " 'Call Me Paul': The Long, Hot Summer of Paul Green and Richard Wright." *Mississippi Quarterly* 61.4 (2008): 517–38.

Campbell, Ouida. "Bigger Is Reborn." *Carolina Magazine*, October 1940: 21–23.

Green, Paul. Paul Green Papers, Southern Historical Collection. Wilson Library, University of North Carolina Library, University of North Carolina at Chapel Hill.

———, and Richard Wright. *Native Son*. Unpublished manuscripts of early drafts. North Carolina Collection. Wilson Library, University of North Carolina at Chapel Hill.

———, and Richard Wright. *Native Son (The Biography of a Young American): A Play in Ten Scenes*. New York: Harper, 1941.

Houseman, John. *Run-Through: A Memoir*. New York: Simon and Schuster, 1972.

Kronenberger, Louis. "The Tragic Saga of Bigger Thomas Makes Vivid Theater." *PM* [New York], 25 March 1941: 21.

Lockridge, Richard. "Richard Wright's 'Native Son' Is Offered at the St. James Theater." *New York Sun*, 25 March 1941: 16.

Mantle, Burns, ed. *The Best Plays of 1940–41 and the Year Book of the Drama in America*. New York: Dodd, Mead, 1941.

Reynolds, Paul. Letter to Paul Green, 25 June 1940. Paul Green Papers, Southern Historical Collection, #03693. Wilson Library, University of North Carolina at Chapel Hill.

———. Letter to Paul Green, 2 Apr. 1940. Paul Green Papers, Southern Historical Collection, #03693. Wilson Library, University of North Carolina at Chapel Hill.

Rowley, Hazel. *Richard Wright: The Life and Times.* New York: Holt, 2001.

Scott, Curtis R. "The Dramatization of *Native Son:* How 'Bigger' Was Reborn." *Journal of American Drama and Theatre* 4.3 (1992): 5–41.

Wright, Ellen. Letter to Paul Green, 4 Sept. 1978. Paul Green Papers, Southern Historical Collection, #03693. Wilson Library, University of North Carolina at Chapel Hill.

Wright, Richard. "How 'Bigger' Was Born." In *Native Son,* 431–62. New York: Harper, 2005.

———. Letters to Paul Green, 3 Oct., 1940 and 12 Feb. 1941. Paul Green Papers, Southern Historical Collection #03693. Wilson Library, University of North Carolina at Chapel Hill.

———. *Native Son.* New York: Harper, 1940.

———. "The Problem of the Hero," Richard Wright Papers, Yale Collection of American Literature. Beinecke Rare Book and Manuscript Library, Yale University.

Wynn, Rhoda. Interview with Paul Green. Southern Oral History Program Collection, Southern Historical Collection. Wilson Library, University of North Carolina at Chapel Hill, 1974.

Kaufman, "That Better Way to Find"

Avery, Laurence G., ed. *A Southern Life: Letters of Paul Green, 1916–1981.* Chapel Hill: University of North Carolina Press, 1994.

Carter, Timothy, ed. *Johnny Johnson: A Play with Music in Three Acts.* Critical Edition. New York: Kurt Weill Foundation for Music, 2012.

Carter, Timothy. Program notes. Chicago Folks Operetta production of *Johnny Johnson,* 2017. https://folksoperetta.org/event/johnny-johnson/.

Crawford, Cheryl. *One Naked Individual: My Fifty Years in the Theatre.* Indianapolis, IN: Bobbs-Merrill, 1977.

Green, Paul. *Johnny Johnson (The Biography of a Common Man).* New York: French, 1937.

———. *Plough and Furrow.* New York: French, 1963.

Mordden, Ethan. *Love Song: The Lives of Kurt Weill and Lotte Lenya.* New York: St. Martin's, 2012.

Review of *Johnny Johnson.* Chicago Premiere/Music by Kurt Weill. *Folks Operetta.* https://folksoperetta.org/2017/07/28/johnny-johnson-reader-review/.

Wilson, Woodrow. "Joint Address to Congress Leading to a Declaration of War Against Germany." National Archives and Records Administration, 2 Apr. 1917. https://www.archives.gov/milestone-documents/address-to-congress-declaration-of-war-against-germany.

Owen, "Paul Green and James Boyd"

Avery, Laurence G., ed. *A Southern Life: Letters of Paul Green, 1916–1981*. Chapel Hill: University of North Carolina Press, 1994.

Boyd, James. "Black Injustice." *The Pilot*, 6 Aug. 1943: 2.

———. "Bloodhound." *Scribner's*, Aug. 1931: 209–11.

———. "Our Common Heritage." *The Pilot*, 9 Jan. 1942: 2.

———. "Strategy for Negroes." *The Nation*, 26 June 1943: 884–87.

Brower, Roderick. Personal interview. 20 Jan. 2023.

Butler, Bion H. "In Bygone Days: Twenty Years Ago." *The Pilot*, 26 Aug. 1949: 2.

———. *Old Bethesda at the Head of Rockfish*. New York: Grosset & Dunlap, 1933.

Case, Bill. "Our Katharine." *PineStraw Magazine*, Feb. 2018. https://pinestraw mag.com/our-katharine/.

Cayton, Horace R. "The Negro's Challenge." *The Nation*, 3 July 1943: 10–12.

Green, Paul. *In Abraham's Bosom*. New York: Samuel French, 1927.

———. "Introduction." In *Eighteen Poems* by James Boyd, ix–xiv. New York: Scribner's, 1944.

Hall, Jacquelyn Dowd. Interview with Paul Green. Southern Oral History Program Collection, Southern Historical Collection. Wilson Library, University of North Carolina at Chapel Hill, 1975.

Hyde, Nelson C. "The Pilot Launched in Vass 20 Years Ago." *The Pilot*, 6 Dec. 1940: 5.

Jones, Howard Mumford. *Letters of Sherwood Anderson*. New York: Little, Brown, 1953.

"May Plan 'Old Slave Day' Here During Winter." *The Pilot*, 29 Sept. 1933: 1.

"Memory of James Boyd Is Honored as North Carolina Wing Is Given to Town." *The Pilot*, 8 Apr. 1949: 17.

Norris, Hoke. "New Boyd Tales Reveal Spirit of South." *The Pilot*, 17 Oct. 1952: 2.

Ripley, Katharine B. *Sand in My Shoes*. New York: Brewer, Warren & Putnam, 1931.

Southern Pines Town Council Minutes. 10 Feb. 1931.

"Straws in an Evil Wind." *The Pilot*, 21 July 1944: 2.

Whisnant, David. "Boyd's Influence as Writer, Citizen Widely Noted On 20th Anniversary of His Death." *The Pilot*, 5 March 1964: 9.

———. *James Boyd*. New York: Twayne, 1972.

Williamson, Walter. "Walter Williamson Rallies to Defense Old Slaves Day." *The Moore County News*, 23 Apr. 1936: 6.

Hudson, "Love Is the Soul of Man"

Avery, Laurence G., ed. *A Southern Life: The Letters of Paul Green, 1916–1981.* Chapel Hill: University of North Carolina Press, 1994.

Cotten, Sallie Southall. *The White Doe: The Fate of Virginia Dare, An Indian Tale.* Philadelphia: Lippencott, 1901.

Dawson, Scott. *The Lost Colony and Hatteras Island.* Charleston, SC: History Press, 2020.

Hudson, Marjorie. *Searching for Virginia Dare: A Fool's Errand.* Wilmington, NC: Coastal Carolina Press, 2002.

Lawson, John. *A New Voyage to Carolina.* Chapel Hill: University of North Carolina Press, 1967.

White, John. "The Fourth Voyage Made to Virginia, with Three Shippes, in the Yeere, 1587. Wherein Was Transported the Second Colonie." *The Roanoke Voyages, 1584–1590: Documents to Illustrate the English Voyages to North America under the Patent Granted to Walter Raleigh in 1584.* 2 vols. Ed. David Beers Quinn. New York: New Dover, 1991 (orig. ed., London: Hakluyt Society, 1955), 2: 515–38.

CONTRIBUTORS

Margaret D. Bauer is the Rives Chair of Southern Literature in the Department of English, a Distinguished Professor of Harriot College of Arts and Science, and the editor of the *North Carolina Literary Review* at East Carolina University. In 2017, she received the North Carolina Award for Literature. In 2018, the North Carolina Humanities Council presented her with the John Tyler Caldwell Award. She is vice president of the Paul Green Foundation.

Born in Lumberton, North Carolina, **Synora Hunt Cummings** grew up and currently resides in Johnston County, North Carolina, with her husband, three children, and English bulldog. She is an enrolled member of the Lumbee Tribe of North Carolina. She enjoys working as a school counselor and volunteering in her Native community. When she is not busy serving others, she enjoys baking elaborate cakes, back porch sitting, and traveling with her family.

Georgann Eubanks is the author of five books from the University of North Carolina Press, including the three-volume *Literary Trails* series commissioned by the North Carolina Arts Council. Since 2000 she has been a principal with Donna Campbell in Minnow Media, LLC, an Emmy-winning multimedia company creating independent documentaries. She has also published short stories, poems, reviews, and profiles in journals including *Oxford American*, *Southern Review*, *Southern Cultures*, and *North American Review*. Eubanks is a past chair of the North Carolina Humanities Council and the North Carolina Literary and Historical Association. She holds the part-time position of literary executor and executive director of the Paul Green Foundation.

Ian Finley earned an MFA in dramatic writing from New York University's Tisch School of Performing Arts, where he received the Harry Kondoleon Award for playwriting. He served as the resident playwright for Burning Coal Theatre Company in Raleigh, North Carolina, for eight years, focused on writing plays with a special relationship to the American South. In 2013 for EbzB Productions, Finley wrote the play *Native* about the 1941 Broadway collaboration of Paul Green and Richard Wright. The play has since been adapted into the film *The Problem of the Hero*, which premiered at the Santa Fe Film Festival in 2023.

Jim Grimsley was born in rural eastern North Carolina and was educated at the University of North Carolina at Chapel Hill, studying writing with Doris Betts and Max Steele. He has published short stories and essays in various quarterlies, including *New Orleans Review*, *Carolina Quarterly*, the *New Virginia Review*, the *Los Angeles Times*, and the *New York Times Book Review*. Jim's first novel *Winter Birds* was published in the United States by Algonquin Books in the fall of 1994. *Winter Birds* won the Sue Kaufman Prize for best first novel from the American Academy of Arts and Letters and was a finalist for the PEN/Hemingway Award. He has published other novels, including *Dream Boy*, *Kirith Kirin*, and *My Drowning*. His books are available in nine languages. He has also published a collection of plays and a memoir, *How I Shed My Skin*. His body of work as a prose writer and playwright was awarded the Academy Award in Literature from the American Academy of Arts and Letters in 2005. For twenty years he taught writing at Emory University in Atlanta. His most recent book, *The Dove in the Belly*, is a love story set in Chapel Hill, published in 2022 by Levine Querido.

Lynden Harris is the founder and director of Hidden Voices, an arts collective that collaborates with underrepresented communities to create performances, exhibits, and media that explore difficult social issues. She is the editor of *Right Here, Right Now: Life Stories from America's Death Row* (Duke University Press, 2021). When she sent copies of the book, along with a letter, she received responses that give her hope that change might at last be possible. The book now has a study guide for small groups. Perhaps we will see the end of this story in our lifetimes.

Marjorie Hudson was born in small-town Illinois, grew up in Washington, D.C., and now lives in North Carolina. Her works include *Indigo Field*, a novel (Regal House Publishing, 2023); *Accidental Birds of the Carolinas*, stories, shortlisted for the PEN/Hemingway Award; and *Searching for Virginia Dare*, a North Carolina Arts Council Notable Book. A 2012 North Carolina Arts Council Fellowship recipient, Hudson teaches creative writing and advocates for wider appreciation of enslaved poet George Moses Horton, who sold his poems to buy his freedom. Her MFA in creative writing is from Warren Wilson College.

Debra Kaufman is the author of the poetry collections *God Shattered*, *Delicate Thefts*, *The Next Moment*, and *A Certain Light*, as well as three chapbooks, many monologues and short plays, and five full-length plays. She produced her play *Harbor Hope* in Durham, North Carolina, and *Illuminated Dresses*, monologues by thirteen women, in Raleigh, North Carolina. She recently adapted *Johnny Johnson*, Paul Green's 1936 antiwar play, and serves on the board of the Paul Green Foundation. http://www.Debrakaufman.info

Novelist and short story writer **Jill McCorkle** was raised in Lumberton, North Carolina. She graduated from the University of North Carolina at Chapel Hill in 1980, where she studied with Max Steele, Lee Smith, and Louis D. Rubin. She also attended Hollins College, now Hollins University, where she received her MA. She is the author of eleven books—four story collections and seven novels—five of which have been selected as *New York Times* Notable Books. She is the winner of the New England Book Award, the John Dos Passos Prize for Excellence in Literature, and the North Carolina Award for Literature.

Ray Owen is a Sandhills native, filmmaker and writer from Southern Pines, North Carolina. He wrote the text for "Bleeding Pines Oratorio" by composer David Serkin Ludwig, dean of music at the Juilliard School. His work has been presented in Northern Ireland and in the U.S. by the Brooklyn Art Song Society, Ravinia Steans Music Institute, Symphony Tacoma, and the University of North Carolina School of the Arts. He has been a contributor for various Sandhills-area publications and has written for the Cultural Landscape Foundation in Washington, D.C. Prior to the founding of Friends of Weymouth in the 1970s, Owen became best friends with John Dowd, son of Weymouth caretaker Robert Dowd, and he came to know Weymouth as a part of his life.

Phillip Shabazz is a poet, writer, and arts educator. He is the author of three poetry collections, *Freestyle and Visitation*, *XYZoom*, and *Flames in the Fire*. He is also the author of a novel in verse, *When the Grass Was Blue*. His forthcoming collection of poetry is titled *Young Hearts, Old Souls*. His poetry has been included in the anthologies *Literary Trails of the North Carolina Piedmont: A Guidebook* and *Home Is Where: African-American Poetry from the Carolinas*. His work has also been published in dozens of journals including *Across the Margin*, *Fine Lines*, *Galway Review*, *Hamilton Stone Review*, *Ham Lit*, *Obsidian*, and *Louisville Review*.

Mike Wiley is a North Carolina–based actor, playwright, and director of multiple one-man documentary dramas and full-cast ensemble plays, including *Leaving Eden*, *The Parchman Hour*, *Downrange: Stories from the Homefront*, *Dar He: The Story of Emmett Till*, the theatrical adaptation of *Blood Done Sign My Name*, and more. Wiley has an MFA from the University of North Carolina at Chapel Hill and was the 2010 and 2014 Lehman Brady Visiting

Joint Chair Professor in Documentary Studies and American Studies at Duke University and the University of North Carolina at Chapel Hill. He has also appeared on Discovery Channel, The Learning Channel, and National Geographic Channel.

Kathryn Hunter Williams received her B.F.A from the University of North Carolina School of the Arts and her M.F.A from the University of North Carolina at Chapel Hill. As a member of PlayMakers Repertory Company, she has performed in *Hamlet*, *The Skin of Our Teeth*, *Everybody*, and *Skeleton Crew*. She has also worked with Living Stage, the Negro Ensemble Company, Manhattan Class Company, and New Dramatist. Kathryn serves as chair of the University of North Carolina Department of Dramatic Art and is the performance director for HiddenVoices, a nonprofit dedicated to bringing life-changing stories into a public forum.

Want to learn more about North Carolina playwright Paul Green?

You can watch filmmaker Hannah Bowman's 2024 documentary,
The Playmaker, about the life and work of Paul Green
on the live streaming services of PBS North Carolina.

Use this QR code to reach the PBS App.

At this site you will find information about the app
and how to download it for a variety of platforms.

You may also visit https://www.pbsnc.org/watch/pbs-app/.

Printed in the USA
CPSIA information can be obtained
at www.ICGtesting.com
JSHW080213290624
65576JS00004B/8